VISIONS OF THE OTHER

Studies in Judaism and Christianity

Exploration of Issues in the Contemporary Dialogue Between Christians and Jews

Editor in Chief for
Stimulus Books
Helga Croner

Editors
Lawrence Boadt, C.S.P.
Helga Croner
David Dalin
Leon Klenicki
John Koenig
Kevin A. Lynch, C.S.P.
Richard C. Sparks, C.S.P.

A STIMULUS BOOK

VISIONS OF THE OTHER

Jewish and Christian Theologians Assess the Dialogue

**Edited by
Eugene J. Fisher**

A STIMULUS BOOK

PAULIST PRESS ◆ NEW YORK ◆ MAHWAH

Library of Congress Cataloging-in-Publication Data

Visions of the other: Jewish and Christian theologians assess the dialogue / edited by Eugene J. Fisher.
    p.   cm. — (Studies in Judaism and Christianity) (A Stimulus book)
    Includes bibliographical references and index.
    ISBN 0-8091-3477-2 (pbk.)
    1. Judaism—Relations—Christianity—1945- —Congresses. 2. Christianity and other religions—Judaism—1945- —Congresses. 3. Judaism (Christian theology)—Congresses. I. Fisher, Eugene J. II. Series.
BM535.V54   1994
261.2′6—dc20   94-18416
                                                      CIP

Published by Paulist Press
997 Macarthur Boulevard
Mahwah, New Jersey 07430

Printed and bound in the United States of America

Contents

Acknowledgements and Dedication

The editor would like to acknowledge the efforts of the local organizing committee for the Ninth National Workshop on Christian-Jewish Relations, held in Baltimore, Maryland in May of 1986, for it was in this setting that these papers (with one exception) were first presented. They have been updated by their authors for this publication. Particular gratitude must be given to Charles and Margaret Obrecht, who have seen to it that the spirit of the National Workshop they so ably hosted has been embodied in an ongoing Institute for Jewish-Christian Studies in Baltimore, and to Dr. James Brashler of St. Mary's University in Baltimore, who began the editing process for this volume. As always, this book is an expression of my love for my wife, Cathie, and my daughter, Sarah. This work is dedicated to the memory of two great pioneers of the dialogue, who passed away during its preparation: Dr. Claire Huchet Bishop and Msgr. John Oesterreicher. May their memory be blessed.

Introduction

Eugene J. Fisher

Jews and Christians stand today at the end of an often tragic but always linked history. What are the implications for the third millennium of the renewed vision of dialogue that is possible just a generation after the light from the fires of the crematoria of Auschwitz set in new perspective the human capacity for evil? What, after all our shared history, do we Jews and Christians have to say, theologically and morally, to and perhaps equally importantly about one another?

In the past we Christians developed a set of presumptions so negative about the Jewish people and Jewish faith that it has justly been called a "teaching of contempt." Built upon the curious and logically indefensible notion of collective Jewish guilt for the death of Jesus (because some Jews were, historically, involved in the events, all Jews then and now were "guilty"), the ancient teaching of contempt soon began to see in Jewish suffering a sort of inverted "proof" of the Christian theological understanding of Jesus. Jews suffered, it was opined, because God was angry at them for "rejecting" and killing Jesus. The fact that most Jews would never have heard of Jesus in his lifetime, much less been in a position to accept or reject him, and the fact that most Jewish suffering was caused by Christians, of course, were not considered relevant to the circular reasoning of the supersessionist theory. Likewise, little reflection was given to the fact that if God could break the "everlasting" covenant (to use the consistent biblical phrase) with the Jewish people for alleged moral or other failings, God's faithfulness to the Church is also called into question because of the sins of Christians.

So widespread was supersessionism among Christians over the centuries that it was virtually never questioned. No ecumenical council recognized by Catholicism, Protestantism or Orthodox Christianity, therefore, ever took it

1

up as an issue. Interestingly, then, when the Second Vatican Council and other Christian bodies began in the mid-twentieth century to ponder the Church's relationship with the Jewish people, the very first official and doctrinally relevant statements since apostolic times were issued.

Today, three decades after the Second Vatican Council (and a bit more after some of the earlier Protestant statements following World War II), we are in effect in the second generation of a theological dialogue between the Church and the Jewish people made possible by the elimination of Christian claims to have replaced Judaism in God's plan of salvation. We stand in a unique moment of history, reassessing all that has gone before us in a spirit of reconciliation and renewed hope for the future. Much is at stake, for good or ill, in how we today understand and frame Christian-Jewish relations.

The four major papers included here were originally delivered at the 9th National Workshop on Christian-Jewish Relations in Baltimore in 1986. They have been reviewed by the authors for publication in this volume. To them have been added a brief bibliography and an update of developments in Baltimore.

In this book, four of the most important scholar-theologians in the world attempt to grapple with questions of ultimate evil and—perhaps even more difficult to grasp—potential goodness. The four essays form an extended dialogue between four compassionate and sensitive searchers. In the perspectives of the death of the Holocaust and the rebirth of the Jewish story in the ingathering of the Jews in the land of Israel, they ask how are we to frame (or, rather, reframe) our traditional understandings of God, evil, human freedom, and the morality of power? How, in the light of these new chapters in the history of God's people, Jews and Christians, are we to tell our own stories while taking into account the divinely charged reality of the other's story?

John Pawlikowski of the Catholic Theological Union in Chicago surveys the major Jewish and Christian theologians grappling in our generation with the immense significance of this closely interrelated set of contemporary theological issues. Most helpfully, he responds directly as a Christian to major aspects of the thought of the two Jewish thinkers included here.

Anyone who is aware of the long, complex and often tragic history of Jewish-Christian relations (see the companion volume to this one, *Interwoven Destinies: Jews and Christians through the Ages*, Paulist Press, Stimulus Books, 1993), cannot but feel a deepening sense of excitement as the present dialogue of two Christian and two Jewish scholars of our own time proceeds. The disputations of the past, in which our scholars traditionally came together only to "prove" the superiority of their own views, are here eclipsed by a larger task, undertaken by four voices sharing and working together. This is, perhaps, the greatest surprise. Out of the polemical dissonances of the past there now emerges a chorus beginning to find its proper harmonies. The voices do not sing only one melody, of course, because the basic perspectives are unique and will not admit of syncretism. But they complement each other in surprising ways.

Rabbi Irving Greenberg offers an "organic" model of Jewish-Christian relations. Its basic outlines are drawn equally from the heart of Jewish tradition and from the questions raised by the Shoah for Jews and Christians alike. While some of its images of Christianity will not, as Pawlikowski points out, be wholly acceptable to Christians, Greenberg's essay moves reflection on the central issues of the dialogue a qualitative step forward beyond the thought of Martin Buber and Franz Rosenzweig. Many in Baltimore at the 9th National Workshop on Christian-Jewish Relations, at which these papers were first presented, it can be said, felt that they were privileged to participate in an historic moment in hearing this presentation.

In Christian reflection on the implications of the Church's contemporary encounter with a renewed Jewish people, van Buren provides a fitting summation of the Christian side of the ancient and ever present journey to dialogue traveled in this volume. In defining the present state of the question for Christians, he challenges other Christians to move beyond his own efforts.

Finally, Rabbi David Hartman of Jerusalem offers a glimpse of what the dialogue of the future might be like as it works toward a mature sense of religious pluralism. As a Jew living in Jerusalem, Hartman approaches the dialogue with Christianity from an historically unique stance, in the modern State of Israel, in which it is Christians rather than Jews who are in the minority. Like Pawlikowski, Greenberg, and van Buren, Hartman focuses on human freedom and power, and on the responsibilities of covenant in our time. His, too, is a vision that cannot be encapsulated in a summary introduction such as this one. His concluding remarks breathtakingly apply an ancient rabbinic dictum, "these and these alone are the words of the living God," to the centuries-long debate between Jews and Christians over the proper interpretation of Sacred Scripture. It at once summarizes all that has been said and opens up to us new horizons of mutual reflection.

It is the call of the living God, after all, that is the real point of this volume and of the dialogue itself. Herein lies our ultimate foundation of hope and our ultimate religious mandate to pursue the dialogue despite its manifest risks and uncertainties. The present generation has within its power not only to destroy the world but to reshape the whole of our previous relationships along new and surprising ways. That reshaping may well provide a model of hope not only for Jews and Christians, but for all humanity.

Pentecost/Shavouth
1994/5754

JEWS, CHRISTIANS AND
A THEOLOGY FOR TODAY

Judaism and Christianity: Their Respective Roles in the Strategy of Redemption

Rabbi Irving Greenberg

From the time that Judaism and Christianity grew together, matured into separate religions, and separated, until today, the two have had one central message in common: the triumph of life. Both affirm that this is a world grounded in (or created by) God, an infinite source of life, goodness and power. Life is growing and becoming more and more like the God who is its ground. The human being has the qualities of life—freedom, consciousness, relatedness and power—which are the fundamental qualities of God. Because human life possesses these qualities at a level which no other life has, it is the highest form of life and has attained the dignity of being "in the image of God".

As defined by the Talmud, by dint of being in the image of God, each human life has the innate dignity of infinite value, equality, and uniqueness. The task of religion is to uphold the sacredness of the image of God and to nurture its further growth in each human being. Not the least way in which this is accomplished is by relating the human—as individuals and in community—to the God who loves and confirms the human.

With the help of God and the leadership of the religious faithful, the process of perfecting life will go on until the triumph of life takes place. The world itself will be restructured to respect and treat properly the life that is in the image of God. The ultimate result will be triumph over death as well as over all those forces of degradation of life that exist in the world.

To realize this tradition of the triumph of life and the fulfillment of life's "image of God" potential, humanity would have to overcome poverty, hunger, war, oppression, sickness, and even death itself. These worldly goals—as dramatic and even improbable as they may appear—are the necessary infrastructure for the attainment of the ultimate fulfillment. According to both Judaism and Christianity, overcoming the enemies of life will pave the way to the fullest realization of the relationship between God and humanity. In the climax of material, relational, and spiritual wholeness, the fullest depth of life's capacity will be achieved.

By contrast, hungry, starving, oppressed people cannot realize the supreme potential of their life force, nor even the fullest development of relationship and love. While it is true that the poor or the suffering may relate to God out of their agony even more than the affluent and the wealthy, they turn to God in their weakness or suffering. The Jewish dream is that humans establish ultimate relationships—with God and fellow human beings—out of strength and freedom.

ILLUSION, HOPE AND COVENANT

Judaism and Christianity both promise that this vision of perfection, which appears so far from the present reality, will nevertheless come to be. Taken by itself, such a vision sounds in all candor like a fantasy—like an escapist illusion. Indeed, much of modern culture has developed from the growing human conviction that this "fairy tale" is not worth waiting for and that one can and should do something in the present to improve conditions. But neither religion offers itself as a fairy tale; nor are they content to remain a vision. Neither religion claims that the promised land, the final stage of history, is already a fact. Their vision is most accurately described as a hope.

Why is a hope different than an illusion or an escape? Hope is a dream which is committed to the discipline of becoming a fact. Illusions and fantasies do better when one does not try to carry them out. Dreams are often so disappointing when realized that one prefers to cling to the dream rather than risk disillusion. A hope commits itself either to become a fact or to renounce itself and to confess not merely failure but falsity. Thus both religions have staked their truth and their truth claims on making their vision into a fact. Both religions have backed this hope by a commitment to make it happen. The covenant is the pledge to work to realize the dream. This decisive move—the transcendent and the immanent reaching out toward each other—unites the two religions. This unlimited partnership of the divine and the human is the ultimate dimension of religious calling in both traditions.

COVENANT AS DIVINE COMMITMENT TO A HUMAN PROCESS

From the divine perspective, the covenant is nothing less than God's promise that the goal is worthy and will be realized, that humans will be accompanied all the way, and that God will provide an ongoing model of how to be human. The divine initiative elicits a matching response—a human promise to persevere and work until the goal is reached. Both religions teach that the people of Israel, the covenantal people (however each faith defines that), are pledged not only to work but to teach and to model how to be human to the rest of humanity.

There is yet another dimension implied in covenant. Attaining the infinite goals of this vision appears to be beyond finite human capacity. The accomplishments needed appear so transcendent and so remarkable that in a sense only God can accomplish them. Nevertheless, says the Bible, God has made a commitment that the result will not be imposed; it will not be granted by divine fiat. The state of perfection will be accomplished on and through a human scale only. The central point of the covenant process itself is that despite having all the power to do what God chooses, God has chosen to make the divinely desired outcome dependent on human capacities and efforts.

The Bible witnesses that God is voluntarily self-limited. God calls humans into partnership out of love and respect for them. But people do not function in abstractions; they function in the context of other people. They create institutions. They organize themselves in groups to carry out their mission. They function with hierarchies or with "rules of the game." They create committees. This process, too, is affirmed by the divine pledge.

The very fact that God chose to work through committees already shows the ultimate risk taken by the divine! The limitations, frustrations, betrayals—even the surprises and acts that exceed divine expectations—are all implicitly factored into the covenantal process accepted and affirmed by God. The risk is indissolubly attached to the repeatedly renewed divine commitment to work with the people of God and other human messengers within the human context. Both religions testify that no matter what disappointments and anguish have followed, God has remained committed to working through human agency. This means that redemption will take place through humans who are rooted in the natural order. The people of God seek roots in their land, grow attached to their own homeland, identify with particular heroes, relate to a particular family, and create a particular community. Thus redemption takes place within the matrix of human history.

The commitment to covenant also means that redemption will take place at a human pace. It has taken the twentieth century with its revolutionary experiences to make us realize the depth and subtlety of that biblical point. The covenantal dream is revolutionary, but the pace is incremental. Revolutions, if they are to be carried out both humanly and properly, take place incrementally. Humans rarely go more than one step at a time voluntarily. Attempts to force them to go faster—even when the goal is perfection—typically run into normal human resistance to radical change. All too often, those who seek to bring about perfection in one stroke become impatient and oppressive. They decide to eliminate the opposition that is holding up the final breakthrough. Soon a new oppression has been established for the sake of redemption.

This alternate way is the great temptation which saviors—divine and human—always are attracted to: to force the other to be free, to redeem people against their will. This way too often ends up being oppressive because it leads the redeemer to slip into the deepest form of contempt for the very beings that the savior sought to redeem. The contempt grows out of the gap between humans as they are and as the redeemer wants them to be. Thus the logic of redemption corrupts the logic of love itself. By contrast, the divine faithfulness to the principle of working through human agency at a human pace grows out of divine humility and is a statement of profound respect for the human. The acceptance of human limitations is an ultimate act of divine love.

Another implication of this human dimension in the covenant is that God uses human models to bring out the humanness of humans. Moses, David, Rebecca and other biblical figures are all too human models. Christianity's affirmation of Incarnation adds to the Hebrew biblical statement the claim that God so wanted to be a part of the covenantal process that God literally took on human form in order to play another crucial role in the process. If this concept is not carefully controlled, it can undermine the very goal it seeks to advance, viz. the perfection of humans. Triumphalist interpretations of the Incarnation that use it to demean Judaism (i.e. that claim that this is a higher revelation, one beyond the grasp of Judaism's religious categories) tend to devalue the human role in the covenant. Thereby, they destroy the object (human dignity and completion) for whose sake God undertook the whole covenantal process! Giving up the supersessionist interpretations of Incarnation constitutes a Christian recovery of respect for humanity and of the divine respect for humanity.

In its wisest forms, the Christian tradition resisted attempts to totally divinize Jesus. It insisted on his ultimate retention of humanness—even though this created great philosophical problems and paradoxes. The dynamic tension is never resolved because human feelings of adequacy to cope with reality vary from culture to culture. To put it bluntly, whenever humans feel helpless or despair of human inadequacy, they are more likely to focus in on a divinely sent redeemer (or on the Christian claim that God "in person" will bring redemption). In cultures, such a modernity, where the sense of human power grows, the focus on Jesus' humanity grows.

From this perspective, one difference between the two religions can be stated thus: whereas Jewish tradition affirms that the final goals can be attained under the leadership of a human avant-garde, Christianity adds the claim that God became the human model that leads humans into the final state. Thus Christianity also concedes that only a human model can bring out the fullness of humanity. Once the triumphalist distortion is removed, Christians can begin to recognize the Incarnation model is profoundly Jewish, albeit rejected by Judaism. Jews can begin to recognize that the Incarnation concept should not be dismissed as some bizarre import from Hellenistic culture but viewed as an extension of the use of human exemplars to evoke maximum covenantal behavior. It is not that Jews and Christians will accept each other's views on this issue, but they can come to realize that both positions grow out of strategies for achieving the goals of the covenant held in common.

Divine models alone cannot bring out the fullness of humanity because the divine is too great, too overwhelming, too much beyond human experience. When one sees somebody so great that one cannot dream of being that way, it brings out a feeling of insufficiency and guilt. This may lead people to abandon trying to grow altogether. By contrast, seeing a fellow human being beyond one's own current standard brings out the realization that it is possible to do the same. This enlarges one's own potential. For this very reason, Christianity, despite its affirmation of incarnation, remains committed to the use of human models to evoke the response of others. And Judaism *a fortiori* insists on human paradigms.

In an early stage of my own personal religious development, I was struggling with my Jewish heritage and some of the ethical dilemmas and self-criticism generated by encounter with the Holocaust. I hesitated, with great inner conflict, and asked myself whether to question or wrestle with inherited traditional positions. No one wants to be an outsider, and I was especially hesitant because I was deeply rooted in my tradition and I love it. At this critical juncture, I received crucial guidance from Christian thinkers. I saw profoundly Christian thinkers, deeply rooted in their tradition, challenging its inherited traditional positions on Judaism. The model of Christian candor, of Christian self-criticism and integrity in wrestling with ultimate divine values, such as can be seen in the work of thinkers such as Roy Eckardt and Paul van Buren, evoked in me the belief and then the capacity that I could grow and develop beyond myself. If they, as Christians, could hold themselves to the standard of patriarch Jacob, who became Israel by struggling with God and humans, perhaps I as a Jew could do it within my own tradition as well.

FROM GENERATION TO GENERATION: HOPE AND COVENANT

The goal of perfection is "unreal" when it is stated as if it were already true or to be achieved at once. If we understand from the covenantal model that it will be accomplished humanly, we understand that the goal is reached gradually, one generation at a time. I will take it as far as I can go and then I will pass it on to my child. If we pass it on properly and the next generation takes up the task, and the next generation after that, then ultimately, but step by step, redemption is transformed from being a fantasy into a realizable dream. If we persist, if we achieve some piece of the final perfection in every generation and yet never settle for that, then we can go on to perfection itself. This is the incredible tenacity and power of the covenantal commitment.

As long as there is family life or a community (which can pass it on to other generations, even if I personally have no children), then this dream becomes steadily more achievable. When Abraham started, what were the chances of overcoming death? The average life expectancy in the Middle East in Abraham's time is estimated to have been no more than twenty to thirty years of life. Now, a mere 3,500 years later, the average life expectancy in America, at least, is close to eighty years old. If we can triple human life every 3,500 years, to achieve total triumph over death should not be all that difficult! The key is to think in terms of eons, not just in terms of one life-time. The self-directed narcissism of modern life encourages the belief that life ends with one's own life. If we think in terms of the incredible human capacity to pass on the covenant, our chances of final realization are much better than superficial appearances imply.

THE PARADOX AND DIALECTICS OF COVENANT

In accepting human agency and human partnership, God has taken on extraordinary risks. Humans can only hear so much. The greatest of teachers cannot go more than a little beyond his or her students' capacity without losing them. Therefore, the divine word must be self-limited to the extent of human capacity—or perhaps a little beyond. This raises the risk that humans will hear selectively only what they want to hear, i.e. only part of the word of God. Then humans in the very process of carrying out a mission can subvert it.

Along the way, humans may lose sight of the goal. There has to be a community to pass on the covenant from generation to generation. Then what about the natural tendency of communities to love only their own? The message of universal love in the covenant of redemption can easily be turned inward onto the community and lead to a rejection of others. Such inwardness can turn a Gospel of love into a rationalization of hatred, persecution and murder. It can turn a religion that seeks redemption into a family business, conscious only of the need to take care of one's own immediate relatives.

There are many dialectical tensions built into the convenantal structure. There is grace, the divine role in the partnership and the extraordinary initiative of God's love. Yet, the counterpart is the centrality of humans and the fullest participation of the human in the process. When they focus on the aspect of grace, both individuals and communities find it difficult to explore the limits and potential of human participation in covenant. Similarly, if one focuses on continuity in the covenant, it is difficult to plumb the depths of change and transformation in history. If, on the other hand, there is a community that is particularly quick to understand the role of transformation or change, it finds it difficult to adjust to the ongoing validity of tradition. Humans cannot keep the covenantal tensions in perfect balance. The key to upholding the totality of covenant and the fullest realization of the goal is that there be multiple communities working on many roads toward perfection, and there be mutual criticism to keep standards high. Perhaps this is why the divine strategy utilized at least two convenantal communities. Even with Christianity and Judaism both in the world, neither religion has succeeded in bringing the final redemption to its fullest flowering.

Seen from this perspective—dare one say from the perspective of a divine strategy of redemption rather than from within the communities embedded in historical experience and needs?—both religions have more in common than they have been able to admit to themselves. Although they are independently valid faiths, they differ so fundamentally that the traditional record is dominated by bitter conflict; both Judaism and Christianity share the totality of their dreams and the flawed finiteness of their methods. In each religion the dream is revolutionary, but it is embedded in a community and a tradition that work realistically for ultimate realization.

Both Judaism and Christianity dream of total transformation while remaining willing to accept the finitude and limitations of humans and go one step at a time. Both groups persist in preaching their messages despite their difficulties and historical suffering. And despite the terrible history of their relationship, each has witnessed to God and the human covenantal mission in its own way. For what often seems an eternity, both have hoped and waited, and both have transmitted the message and worked for the final redemption.

RESPONSES TO THE HOLOCAUST

In our lifetime, we have lived through the greatest assault in history on this vision of hope and on the covenantal way. The Holocaust was not only a triumph of death. It was the denial of all values to life. It is one thing to kill six million people—a devastating blow to the dreams of life's triumph. But there is a far more radical denial in the Holocaust. Consider the fact that Nazi operatives calculated in 1942 that if they worked the average Jewish prisoner to death over a period of nine months the profit per person was 1,631 RM (Reichsmark) on the average. The profit margin was enhanced by lowering the daily amount of food and by collecting the gold teeth and utilizing the bones and ashes of the cremated prisoners. It is one thing to kill people; it is another thing to number them and turn them into ciphers while they are still alive. That constitutes an active denial of the infinite value and uniqueness of the human.

It is one thing to kill people, but it is another thing to turn them into filth that stinks of excrement. It is one thing to kill Jews, but it is another to cut the asphyxiating gas supply per chamber load in half in 1944 to save money. That decision meant that it took twice as long to die in agony. By 1944, the Nazis had reached the ultimate efficiency. It cost less than one-half penny per person to gas the Jews in 1944. Then it was decided to throw Jewish children alive into the crematorium to save that one-half cent. Such decisions go beyond murder. They are theological decisions, affirmations of anti-values. They deny the image of God. They testify that life is worthless.

Such a successful mass murder and denial of the value of life poses the most radical question. As Richard Rubenstein argued, in such a setting the only Messiah is death. Not the triumph of life but the triumph of death is the most accurate description of human history. In the perspective of Auschwitz, there is no hope. In Auschwitz the whole covenantal way with all its remarkable accomplishments and with all its wonderful contributions to human history is revealed as an illusion.[1] This is the reality that Jews and Christians have lived through in our lifetime. It is the response to that reality which we must focus on now.

How did the two religious communities react to this total assault, this decisive victory for death? The more we reflect upon this response the more we

---

1. I do not mean that both religions have identical problems with the Holocaust. This experience of hopelessness strikes a double blow at Christianity. In addition to the crisis of the unredeemed world which Jews confront, Christianity must confront the fact that it is implicated in creating the context of hatred which made Auschwitz possible. Nevertheless, the central crisis for both grows out of the shattered paradigm of the triumph of life.

realize the wisdom of the divine: to depend on humans after all. Surely one of the great religious moments in history has been revealed in the human response to this overwhelming experience of death.

POWER AND THE RETURN TO HISTORY

Both religions have responded in fundamental faithfulness to the covenant. They have decided to go back into history and to face the challenge. For Jews, this meant the commitment to take power in order to protect and restore the value of life. Jews could not depend on waiting for the Messiah or on God's grace. They had to reassert the value of life by taking power. To restore the image of God in the individual Jew, they had to create a society, and an army, and a political structure that could truly preserve the infinite value of the human. Jews had to build a structure which promised that if in the future a Jew was excluded and isolated as a target for murder or for hunger or for death, there would be an Israeli paratrooper to come into Entebbe, or a Mossad agent who would sneak into Sudan or Ethiopia to take people out of starvation and oppression to life again. Jews knew that in order to take power and to renew the covenant of hope, they had to settle in the land which incarnated the biblical promise of restoration and renewal of the covenant. They had to overcome death with life, which is to say that they had to have children. The overwhelming majority of Jews did not despair of the Messiah, as Rubenstein's logic suggested they should. Rather they despaired of waiting for the Messiah. Since they could not just wait, they decided that they had to take action to bring the Messiah.

Among Christians, similar responses have taken place, although not universally. Among Christians, too, the overwhelming response has been a renewed commitment to redeem the world. The growth of the theology of liberation, with all the problematics it raises, is an affirmation of commitment not to accept life as it is, but to bring closer the final redemption. Christian self-critique and Christianity's commitment to become a gospel of love after serving as a sanctuary of hatred of Jews for two thousand years bespeaks an extraordinary restoration of the purity of the covenant. The Christian search to recapture the human role in the covenant, expressed so powerfully in Vatican II, is an attempt to restore to the Church a partially lost dimension of the role of the people of God and of community in history. Such affirmations of life and hope ought to be celebrated by Jews no less than Christians.

Both religions have made the commitment to take power in order to attempt to restore the credibility of the covenant. To take power in our time is a serious enterprise. It involves a literal *imitatio Dei*. To take power is to become more like God—that capability is also part of the ultimate vision.

Religion can no longer be seen as just a matter of spirituality. Taking power is an imitation of God, just as love is an ultimate identification with God, and just as consciousness is an identification with the divine. All these qualities are characteristics of God.

When humans develop genetic engineering or nuclear power, they are taking on aspects of the power of God. When humans exercise democracy and freedom, they are imitating the power and humanity of God. Any assumption of divine power raises the possibility of idolatry, the risk of making partial human power absolute and using it without limit. Such an idolatrous attitude is evident when people turn nuclear power into world destruction, or genetic engineering into human manipulation. Such abuses turn freedom into license and anarchy, and art into violent pornography. A thousand other abuses are possible under freedom. Since the commitment to take power increases the moral risk for all humanity, one must intensify the demand for covenantal limits, for mutual criticism, and for multiple models. In short, we are more deeply drawn to the need for more than one covenantal community.

THE ETHICS OF POWER AFTER THE HOLOCAUST

The greatest challenge facing both religions today is how to handle the return into history. For Jews, the first step is to develop sufficient power for life. Israel is threatened. Israel needs enough power to protect itself. The first task for a people who are used to living in exile and powerlessness and existing on tolerance is to develop enough strength to stay alive. Israel needs enough power to give full dignity to its citizens. Indeed, every nation needs economic and political power if it is to give full dignity to its citizens. The need to develop adequate power is not yet sufficiently appreciated in the religious communities. Religions still remain nervous that human power will inevitably result in competition with God's power. First, they must learn that the true task is to be like God and to develop power. This effort leads directly to the second challenge: making sure that power exists within the covenantal framework so that it is used appropriately.

Both religions face the urgent need to develop an ethic of power. Power does corrupt. Therefore, humanity is always in need of great help to avoid the cancerous corruption that grows as power grows exponentially. For example, Israel needs help to make sure that its citizens participate fully, that it not abuse its Arabs, and that it will not lose sight of its own humanity in defending itself against those who would kill it. That is why both Israel and other communities need all the ethical resources that religion can bring to them.

To prevent power from becoming abusive, both communities need to draw on any other source in society beyond religion that can help them. Jews must learn how to handle openness and freedom so that the process will not lead to assimilation or to disappearance. Jews need to learn how to use the freedom which they now possess wisely rather than to use its license to attack each other and delegitimate each other. Such internal abuse is something Jews were afraid to inflict on each other when they were afraid of Gentiles. Today, with comfort, security and power in their hands, there is a real risk that Jews will split apart into multiple communities at war with one another.

As Jews discover their own power, they will in turn be enabled to discover the Gentile, the Christian, as an image of God. Such a discovery can only come because of the dignity and mutual encounter made possible by a democratic society. When Jews were persecuted ghetto dwellers, they knew the Gentile only as the inhuman enemy. The human dimension and the fullest religious dignity of Christians can only be discovered through dialogue. Jews today are struggling with a new dialectic of universalism and particularism. The protection of the particular, which is a paramount concern throughout Jewish history, is being corrected to overcome the hostility of centuries which led to a cultural demeaning of Gentiles and of Christianity. General rejection and negative stereotyping was a very normal human reaction. It represents in-group morality and defensiveness in response to Christian oppression and persecution of Jews. In a situation of power and acceptance, however, one cannot allow the same dismissal of the other. In short, Jews today must learn to strike a balance between Jewish needs, as urgent and as difficult as these are, and Jewish contributions and obligations to the general society. Jews need both to be themselves and to participate alongside others for the sake of the larger vision.

JEWISH-CHRISTIAN DIALOGUE: THE NEXT STAGE

Let us apply these principles to Jewish-Christian dialogue. There can be no Judaism without Jews. Therefore, Christians must stop attempting to grow by missionizing Jews. Beyond merely ending proselytizing activities among Jews, Christians need to go after the antisemitism that is the residue of their own teachings. Antisemitism is the most ubiquitous, worldwide, permanent moral infection of human history. Sometimes one despairs of overcoming it. It has now spread worldwide, even in countries where there are no, or hardly any Jews such as in Japan - all this by propaganda emanating from Russia and the radical Arab countries as well as from fundamentalist Christians.

It is not enough to stop teaching about Jews as "killers of Christ." The deeper challenge is to go back and uproot the very sources of the contagion which continue to pour this virulent infection into humanity's bloodstream. Christians must make sure that the Christian breakthroughs in understanding

Judaism are transmitted and taught on the mass level. The morally and theologically remarkable work done by Christians in the dialogue of the last twenty years has one serious weakness. It remains basically the possession of a minority of inspired people. It is not yet understood properly at the mass level and not yet dominant at the upper decision-making levels.

Christians need to learn to take worldly holiness and liberation seriously without slipping into romanticizing the third world. Usually, that way ends up with the Christians viewing Israel and American Jews negatively. Such a "romantic" Christian worldview is a real possibility in Christian thought today. Christians are used to seeing Jews as the oppressed and as paradigms of powerlessness. Jews have traditionally played such a role in the Christian imagination, as for example in the "wandering Jew" motif in western literature. What will Christianity do with Jews who have achieved power, as in Israel, or economic success, as in the United States? Will Jews now become the symbol of bourgeois wealth?

All these issues represent valid Jewish concerns after the Holocaust, but it would be self-indulgent for Jews to stop there in the dialogue. As Jews work with Christians, they will discover the ethical power of Christianity, the religious depth of its liturgical life, and the extraordinary effects of its religious models, even the models that are most remote from Jewish perception of the past 1,800 years. In so doing, Jews will begin to discover the positive aspects of Christian "otherness." Jews will have to fight the patronizing tendency to discover Christianity as a wonderful religion only because it is so similar to Judaism. A more searching understanding of Christianity needs to be developed and articulated by the Jewish community today.

TOWARD A JEWISH THEOLOGY OF CHRISTIANITY

Authentic Jews deeply rooted in their own tradition must struggle to do justice to the organic relationship of Judaism and Christianity. Jews must confront the fact that the separation and the career of Christianity, as painful, as bloody, and as ugly as it has been vis-à-vis Judaism, cannot simply be dismissed as a deviation from covenant history. Historically, Jews have been reluctant to admit the possibility of partnership. While there is both risk (that Christian fundamentalists could abuse such recognitions to try to missionize Jews) and resistance (from Jews who fear that the minority's survival is endangered if there is greater openness and respect for the majority culture), this is a time for heroic measures to advance the cause of redemption. This has ever been the proper covenantal response to great setbacks in history.

In light of the Holocaust, Jews must develop a theology of non-Jewish religions that will articulate their full spiritual dignity. One cannot simply treat them as pale reflections of Judaism. A new theology is ethically necessary. As we learned from the Holocaust, when one treats others as having less spiritual dignity than oneself, the temptation is to stand by when they are physically in danger as well. Theological contempt cannot be separated from human responsibility. It is hard enough to risk your life to save somebody you look up to and admire. It is almost impossible to do it for someone you think is intellectually dense or spiritually inferior. The tradition of spiritual contempt led many Christians to abandon Jews in the Holocaust. Jews who have suffered this indignity in the past must strive harder not to be guilty of similar misjudgments. "What is hateful to you, do not do to others." This is the summary of the whole Torah according to our master Hillel.

Secondly, Jews must develop the ability to recognize the full implications of the truth that the Lord has many messengers. While it is true that Jews have always believed that there is salvation for the individual outside of Judaism, this generality does not do justice to the full spiritual dignity of others who, after all, live their lives in religious communities, and not just as individuals.

Finally, given human limitations and the corrupting effect of power, only the wide distribution of political, cultural, and theological power can insure the safety of the world. A moral balance of power is the best guarantor of moral behavior. It follows that Jews need the presence of Christianity and other religions, as religions need the presence of secular movements, to prevent any one group from attaining societal domination which can lead to oppression. Thus the presence of many spiritual power centers will enable humanity to move toward the creation of the kingdom of God.

Here then are some thoughts from a Jewish perspective on taking Christianity seriously as a religion on its own terms as well as on our own.

EXODUS, MESSIAH AND RESURRECTION

Both religions grow out of the Exodus. The Exodus is a fundamental event of liberation, which points beyond itself to further redemptions. The prophets understood this clearly. If the dream is the ultimate triumph of life, then the Exodus is not the end. It is the beginning of the process. The test of Judaism's vitality is that it will continue to generate further movements toward Messianic redemption. As long as Judaism generates Messiahs, one can be certain that it is alive.

When Judaism stops generating Messiahs, it is no longer faithful to its own tradition. That does not mean that every Messiah is the final one or even a true one. It does mean that the Messianic impulse is a fundamental test of Judaism's own integrity. In that sense, Christianity is not a mere deviation or misunderstanding; it is an organic outgrowth of Judaism itself.

Contrary to what most modern Jews think, the statement of resurrection made by Christianity grows out of authentic Jewish models. In classical Judaism, resurrection is a legitimate hope. Resurrection is the ultimate statement of the triumph of life. Belief in resurrection is at the heart of rabbinic teaching; the Rabbis placed the affirmation of this belief near the head of the central Jewish prayer.

The early Christians, nurtured by this Jewish hope, decided to follow the Jew whom they had experienced as a Messiah. When the other Jews did not accept this conclusion, the Christians were tempted to interpret this rejection as blindness. The Jewish riposte was: "How can you believe in the Messiah when you see the ongoing presence of death and oppression and suffering?" To this Christians answered, "The kingdom of God is within you." To remove the cognitive dissonance of a world still suffering evil and oppression, Christians were tempted to remove the worldly dimension from their vision and to insist that in the spiritual dimension redemption had in fact been achieved. In this way, Christians were motivated to put forth a triumphalist interpretation of their relationship to Judaism: Judaism was the kernel, first stage faith; Christianity was the "true" faith because it raised redemption to the plane of spirit and eternity instead of remaining fixated at the level of the body and temporality. To this spiritual triumphalism, the Jewish response has been that history shows that Jesus was a "false Messiah" and Christianity an other-worldly religion which fails to take concrete history into account.

With the perspective of 1,800 years and of the last fifty, perhaps it is time to reassess the ancient family quarrel between Jews and Christians. Over the centuries, in situations where Jews were trying simply to survive surrounded by a vast majority which was hostile, they could not step back and take a different perspective on the issue. Perhaps it takes the shattering of worlds represented by the Holocaust to allow new thinking. Perhaps it takes the humility of both communities, existing in a modern world in which all individual religions are dwarfed, to admit this.

Jews today need to look at the issue, not just from the internal community vantage point, but from the perspective of the hypothetical divine plan. Assume there is a divine strategy for redeeming the world using human agents; assume it is the divine will that Judaism and Christianity are together in the world; assume that both are ways of affirming both "yet" and "not yet" with regard to redemption. Assume both are true but that both need the other to embody the fullest statement of the covenantal goal and process. What one individual cannot say without being hypocritical or confused, two communities can state as a balance and corrective toward each other.

THE DIALECTICS OF RELIGIOUS CLAIMS

The covenant's dialectical moves of divine grace and human participation provide an example. In Hebrew Scriptures, humans achieve holiness through family and land, within the natural human order. Yet the very emphasis of the covenant on the natural order leads people to naturalize and to domesticate—and even to defeat—the divine claims. So the temporally and spatially rooted Jewish religion needs the universal, landless church perspective as a corrective.

The focus on life and appreciation for the family as the context for the covenant is distinctively Jewish. But no religion which is strong in one pole of the dialectic is likely to do full justice to the other aspect. To preserve the balance, Judaism needs a religion determined to explore the fullness of death, to explore what it would mean to break out of the family model and create a universal self-defined belief group. Judaism has brought humans even more powerfully into participation in the covenant process (compare the passivity of the biblical temple pilgrim with the activity of the rabbinic Jewish individuals praying in the synagogue); it needs a counterpart religion that is prepared to explore the element of grace and transcendence in a more central way. Each tradition, to be faithful to its own vision, needs the other in order to correct and to exemplify the fullness of the divine-human interaction. In this perspective, each one's experience, Jewish covenant peoplehood and the Christian faith community, is not only validated, it is seen as a necessary expression of the plenitude of divine love and the comprehensiveness of the human role in the covenant.

One Christian interpretation of the emergence of their faith has been that Jews have lost the vision. Why? Because Christians have experienced their own chosenness, so they assumed that Jews have lost theirs. But why? Why is God not capable of communicating to Gentiles through sacramental experiences and to Jews through a more natural order? Why insist that new experiences exhaust God's potential? Why insist that any religious experiences however valid, impugn the competence or quality of the other?

The general Jewish position has been that Jesus was a false Messiah. Why? Would it not be more precise to say that a false Messiah is one who teaches the wrong values and who turns sin into holiness? A more accurate description, from a Jewish perspective would be that Jesus was not a "false" but a "failed" Messiah. He has not finished the job but his work is not in vain.[2]

---

2. Since the religion in his name persecuted Jews, spread hatred and degraded Judaism, the term *false* Messiah was well earned. The term *failed* Messiah recognizes that for hundreds of millions, Christianity was, and is, a religion of love and consolation, i.e. the right values. Use of the

Of course, Christians will hesitate to accept this definition—as will Jews, perhaps more so. Christians will be deeply concerned: Is this a dismissal of Jesus? Does this term demean classic Christian affirmations of Jesus' messiahship and the incarnation? Jews will be concerned: Is this a betrayal of the classic Jewish insistence that the Messiah has not yet come? Does this term breach Judaism's self-respecting boundary which excludes Christian claims?

I believe that none of these fears are warranted. The term "failed Messiah" is an example of the kind of theological language we should be seeking to develop in the dialogue, for it allows for a variety of Christian and Jewish self-understanding. Some Christians will translate this term into their view of Jesus as a proleptic Messiah. Others will insist on their own traditional understanding of Jesus' Messiahship, but will see in the term a divinely willed, much needed spur to believers to confront the fact that the world is not yet perfect and that their task is unfinished. Other Christians who insist on Jesus' Trinitarian status will hear the phrase "failed Messiah" as a reminder that God's self-presentation is deeply humble, not triumphalist. God is identified with the weak and the defeated and with the power of persuasion by model rather than victory by intimidation. Some Jews will read this term as a description of Jesus' actual role in Jewish history; others will understand it as an affirmation of the Jewish "no" to all claims to finality in this unredeemed world. Still others will understand the term as a tribute to Jesus' extraordinary accomplishments, since under the impact of his model, a major fraction of humanity has been brought closer to God and to redemption.

Is not calling Jesus a failed Messiah a form of damning with faint praise? No. Such failures are the key to success of the divine strategy of redemption. If one understands covenantally that human life does not end in one lifetime, then the meaning of failure is even more ambiguous—and in this case, positive.

Christianity has held a supersessionist view of history. The Christian interpretation of the destruction of the Second Temple saw it as the divine refutation of Judaism. Little did Christians realize that even in this ugly interpretation of Jewish history, one designed to obliterate the Jews, they were pursuing a deeply Jewish hermeneutic by interpreting history as the carrier of a divine message. To interpret the destruction of the Temple as in some way a divine call is a recognizably Jewish form of reaction to historical events. By fixing on an outward, triumphalist, and hateful interpretation, Christianity

---

term also presupposes that the religion in his name stops teaching hatred of Jews and becomes a source of healing support for the Jewish people and a purveyor of respect for Judaism. If it continues to nurture stereotypes and hatred of Jews—or if it misuses these more positive views of Christianity in order to missionize Jews—then it proves that Jesus is a false Messiah, after all.

missed a deeper alternative whereby God was calling Jews to a higher level of service in the covenant by ending the Temple sacrifices.

Blinding themselves to the vitality and growth of Jewish tradition, Christians were led to overemphasize the miraculous and the sacramental within Christianity. By distorting Judaism's image and presenting it as a fossil, Christians failed to see the truly innovative form of rabbinic Judaism—its affirmation of covenantal continuity through humans taking more responsibility for the covenant. In Rabbi Joseph B. Soloveitchik's words, through rabbinic response and the development of halacha, humans become co-creators of Torah, the divine word.

By dismissing Judaism as legalism, Christians are tempted not to hear the divine calling that they become more active in the unfolding of the covenantal way. A less triumphalist, more humble Christianity might have interpreted the continuation of Judaism as the divine call to Jews to build on the Hebrew Scriptures and grow into a new level of participation in the covenant. At the same time, Christianity may have been elected to uphold the sacramental dimension of biblical tradition more powerfully.

The Rabbis grasped that the destruction of the Temple was not the end of Judaism. They understood it as the outgrowth of another divine covenantal move, or a self-limiting God acting to call humans to greater participation in the covenant. Some Christians interpreted the destruction of the Temple as divine rejection of Israel. Such an interpretation takes the infinite divine love—whose grace all humans need—and reduces it to the point where it is not adequate to deal with the flaw of the original people of God. If the divine love could not encompass flawed, fallible Jewry even as it reached out to embrace humanity, then how can it be adequate to the task of healing and redeeming all of humankind? And if the original covenant is so fragile and liable to forfeit, then how flimsy is the rock on which the Church is built?

It would have been a more charitable and loving interpretation of God's actions to explain it as a call to the people of Israel to enter exile and to develop an ethic of powerlessness. That ethic preserved the dignity of Jews over the centuries and provided a model for survival in a world of oppression and exile. Inspired by this call, Judaism developed models of halacha that sanctified all of life, not just the holy Temple. Halacha pointed to God in the everyday and in the natural process of history and not just in overt miracles and sacramental incarnations that overwhelmed humans.

Rabbinic tradition accomplished all this not because it failed to recognize "the time of its visitation," but because it was prepared to hear new divine instruction even as it was faithful to the old. Thus rabbinic tradition is profoundly continuous with the Bible while at the same time teaching and concretizing a transformation of the human roles in the covenant. It is not too late for Christianity to learn these models from Jews, even as it is not too late for Jews to focus again on grace and the sacramental and the universal in Christianity. Jews, too, need a corrective lest they lose the richness of the divine will and covenantal dialectic.

AN ORGANIC MODEL FOR JEWISH-CHRISTIAN RELATIONS

Judaism denied the occurrence of divine incarnation; it needed to be authentic to its own religious life. This tempted it to overlook the genuinely Jewish dimension of this Christian attempt to close the gap between the human and the divine. Even while rejecting the model, should Jews not recognize that it grows out of the tormenting persistence of a great distance between the divinely sought perfection and the human condition? One can conceive of a divine pathos that sent not only words across the gap but life and body itself. I say this not as a Jew who accepts this claim, but as one who has come to see that it is not for me to prescribe to God how God communicates to others. Our task is to find ways for humans to hear God. We should measure religions by the criterion of how people act after they hear the word in community. If the Incarnation and Resurrection of Jesus lead to Christian triumphalism, to persecution, and idolatry, then Christianity proves itself to be false. If it leads to deeper compassion and understanding and a grasp of the human realities and human needs and motivated covenantal action, then it validates itself as a channel of the divine.

Both communities are challenged now to see the other without the filters of stereotype and defensiveness. Since we do not own God, we should be grateful for our own religious experiences—and for the experience of others. One can go beyond this not only to an acknowledgement of pluralism, but to an affirmation of the organic nature of the relationship between the two faiths. How else could multiple models be created except in communities which must have their own inner *élan*, their own procedures, their own hierarchy, and their own standard symbols of participation?

One essential implication of the covenant is that there has to be a plurality of legitimate symbols if the divine intention is to raise humans to the fullest capacities of life. The alternative is that there will be only one religion, one's own. It should be the prayer of believers in this time at least, given the power that humans now have, that one's own groups not be the only religion. If indeed we believe that our exclusivity is what God wants, we should be praying that that cup pass from our lips. Perhaps all humans should be praying for the courage and strength to argue with God, and to convince God that humanity will arrive at perfection faster if God follows through on the pluralist implications of the covenantal model.

A PERSONAL WITNESS

In my teaching, I personally continue to affirm the covenant of Israel and the role of the Jewish community as central to God's plans. I proudly assert the remarkable balance of family, tradition, life and vision in Judaism. In the past, I would use as a counterpoint in such presentations the image of Christianity as making unreasonable, otherwordly demands. As a rabbi who has had the chance to have a family, I all too often used celibacy as a counter-model, an example of the lack of humanness in Christianity. Or I would hold up the image of the Cross as a symptom of Christianity's excessive demands. It took years in the Jewish-Christian dialogue before I came to see the extraordinary power of those very models that I was patronizing and dismissing.

I was in Sri Lanka in 1974 for a world dialogue of religions. During the conference, we were taken to visit a local village. There I discovered a group of Christians who had left affluent, successful lives in Scandinavia to dwell in the interior of Sri Lanka to set up a little village for brain-damaged children. Typically, such children were abandoned by their parents to death because in the midst of that poverty, parents could not even take care of healthy children. How moved I was. Here were people who left a life of ease and affluence to go 7,000 miles away to live in poverty and to take care of brain-damaged children. They had to take care of them totally; much of the time they wiped them and changed them. The children could do very little. The caretaker's only reward was to watch the children lie there and moan and look at them. Few children could adequately respond to those who treated them.

Suddenly I was struck by the fact that this unreasonable religion with its incredible demands elicits that kind of response. As a rabbi, I rarely elicited such kinds of behavior—precisely because I did not make "unreasonable" demands. As a rabbi I expected—and accepted—a touch of holiness in everyday activities; I did not anticipate such sacrificial, heroic levels of behavior. In that moment of insight, I realized that my stereotyping dismissals of Christianity had blinded me to one of its greatest religious strengths. Simultaneously, I was tempted into being too reasonable in my expectations of myself and my own community.

To be fair to the Jewish position, it can be argued that perhaps it is more difficult to be a spiritual hero every day in a bourgeois existence than it is to go off and make that kind of lifetime commitment. It may be easier to make self-renouncing moves such as accepting monastic celibacy than to take the daily responsibility and frustration of having to love a wife, or raise a child, or meet a payroll. Having said that, it strikes me that my own Jewishness could grow so much more by taking seriously the sacrificial models offered by Christianity instead of trying to score points at Christian expense.

Christians similarly are tempted to glorify their faith's power and to ignore the fact that Judaism's "normal mysticism" with its strengthening of human models is both profoundly human and deeply religious. Christians have consistently underestimated one of Judaism's greatest triumphs, the halacha, which has hallowed every aspect of life in such brilliant fashion. Typically Christians have dismissed it as tribalism, legalism, or as a lower level of spirituality. The price Christianity paid for this was a persistent loss of worldly spirituality and excessive quietism and asceticism.

Once the triumphalism stops, one discovers that the very themes one dismissed in the other are present in one's own repertoire. Heroic self-sacrifices and spiritual renunciation are profound if less stressed themes in Judaism just as the motifs of going into exile or the peoplehood of those who believe in God are present in Christianity. This is not to say that the two faiths are identical. There are fundamental differences in priorities and method and form as well as in beliefs and history. Yet if one looks carefully, even the differences are nuanced. Major themes in Judaism show up as minor themes in Christianity. Major themes in Christianity, including themes which Jews try to dismiss (such as the kingdom of God as a primary spiritual phenomenon— which is found in the Kabbalah) are in fact important minor themes in Judaism. A much more integral approach would have been to admit from the outset that each group has these tendencies and to deal with them in their natural development. A humbler assessment of our own capacity (coming out of a commitment not to distort or use the covenant for our own purposes) would lead to a more positive attitude toward the other community and willingness to use the other faith as a benchmark to check our own excesses and to learn from the other. Each faith should welcome the other as the spiritual and moral check and balance for the sake of the kingdom which we all seek to create.

CONCLUSION

Both religions have a major task at hand in the generation after the Holocaust. Both religions need to take up the charge of correcting their own deviations from the covenantal way. They need to overcome the denials of the image of God of the other which erode the religious power of each faith tradition. Both have to take up the challenge of developing a liturgical community that can nurture the image of God and thus help humankind avoid being swept into idolatry of secular power. Both communities need the humility of learning from secularism and from each other.

Paradoxically, giving up the stereotypes and hatred, giving up the negative view of the other opens up the risk of assimilation and of losing ourselves.

But we gain the possibility of richness in our own understanding and of an identity that is not dependent on the denial of the other. We act out of weakness to retain the otherness of others because we are afraid we cannot survive choice. Is not the ultimate message of the covenant that God wants us to exercise choice? Models of faith are what we have to gain from each other. Those models evoke our own deepest possibilities.

The power of American society is that those models reach across religious lines. A Christian's self-sacrifice or prophetic self-criticism or a Buddhist's willingness to incinerate himself in defiance of evil can inspire a Jew or a Moslem whose experience is totally different. These models bring out possibilities that I never before saw in myself. Thus as each religion struggles with its own corrupt tendencies it can turn not just inward for help but to other groups for external guidance and inspiration. As David Hartman has suggested, perhaps now that Jews have returned to Israel, they will have enough power and enough self-assurance to face Christians without defensiveness and fear as equals with respect and with deeper understanding.

What will we accomplish by doing this? Both religions can show the world a model of service. Both groups would show that we understand that, as believers, we are channels and vehicles of the divine, not the imperialist owners of God. In a world which kills *en masse* for that which it believes in but is religiously tolerant of people who do not care about religion; in a world where the secular authorities have now killed on a scale to match and surpass the old religious wars, perhaps we can start over again by checking all the stereotypes. Those who glorify the secular and those who glorify the religious can admit that humans own neither God nor other humans. Let the various religious and ethical models shine forth; let us challenge each other to grow and deepen and hear the call of God to advance redemption and to renew the covenant in this generation.

This is a special part of the mission of this generation: to renew revelation, to continue the covenantal way, to discover each other. At least let these two religions model the truth that the love of God leads to the total discovery of the image of God in the other, not to its distortion or elimination. If committed and believing Christians and Jews can discover the image of God in each other, if they can uncover and affirm each one's proper role in the overall divine strategy of redemption, surely the inspiration of this example would bring the kingdom of God that much closer for everyone.

Christian Theological Concerns
After the Holocaust

Dr. John T. Pawlikowski, O.S.M.

In his seminal essay originally presented to the 1974 Cathedral of St. John the Divine Symposium on the Holocaust and contemporary society, Irving Greenberg speaks of the Shoah as an "orienting event" for all future generations.[1] I would basically align myself with this position. It is my firm conviction that, while the Holocaust was multi-causal in nature and had ties with deeply traditional elements in western culture such as Christian antisemitism, it represented a new moment in the history of western society with implications for the future directions of all humankind. While admittedly not everyone who participated in the Holocaust was fully aware of its deepest dynamics, it ultimately represented the beginning of a new era.

With the advent of Nazism the mass extermination of human life in a guiltless fashion became thinkable and technologically feasible. The door was now ajar for an era when dispassionate torture and the murder of millions could become not merely the acts of crazed despots, not merely an irrational outbreak of xenophobic fear, not just a desire for national security, but a calculated effort to reshape history supported by intellectual argumentation from the best and brightest minds in a society. It was an attempt, Emil Fackenheim has said, to wipe out the "divine image" in history. "The murder camp," Fackenheim insists, "was not an accidental by-product of the Nazi empire. It was its essence."[2]

---

1. "Cloud of Smoke, Pillar of Fire: Judaism, Christianity, and Modernity after the Holocaust," in Eva Fleischner (ed.), *Auschwitz: Beginning of a New Era?* New York: Ktav, 1977.

2. *The Jewish Return into History.* New York: Schocken Books, 1978, 246.

For me the fundamental challenge of the Holocaust lies in our altered perception of the relationship between God and humanity and its implications for the basis of moral behavior. What emerges as a central reality from the study of the Holocaust is the Nazi attempt to create the "superperson," to develop a truly liberated humanity, to be shared in only by a select number of people (i.e. the Aryan race). This new humanity would be released from the moral restraints previously imposed by religious beliefs and would be capable of exerting virtually unlimited power in the shaping of the world and its inhabitants. For the Nazis God was dead as an effective force in governing the universe.

To attain their objective the Nazis were convinced that the "dregs of humanity" had to be eliminated or at least their influence on culture and human development greatly curtailed. The Jews fell into this category first and foremost. They were classified as "vermin." But the Poles, the gypsies, gay people and the mentally/physically incapacitated were looked upon as polluters of authentic humanity, as obstacles to the advancement of human consciousness to new levels of insight, power and self-control. Their extermination under the rubric of humankind's purification assumes a theological significance intimately related to the Jewish question. Regrettably the non-Jewish side of the Holocaust has not entered the theological reflections of either Christian or Jewish theologians up till now.[3]

The late Israeli historian Uriel Tal has captured as well as anyone the basic moral challenge of the Shoah. The so-called "Final Solution," he insists, had as its ultimate goal the complete transformation of human values. Its stated intention was the total liberation of humanity from previous moral ideals and codes. When the Nazi program had reached the stage of full implementation, humanity would no longer feel itself bound by the chains of a God concept and its related notions of moral responsibility, redemption, sin and revelation. Nazi ideology sought to transform theological ideas solely into anthropological and political concepts. As Tal has stated the reality of the Nazi perspective,

> God became man, but not in the theological New Testament sense of the Incarnation of the word...or in accordance with Paul's understanding of the

---

3. For some basic information on non-Jewish victims, cf. Bohdan Wytwycky, *The Other Holocaust: Many Circles of Hell.* Washington, DC: The Novak Report, 1980; Frank Rector, *The Nazi Extermination of Homosexuals.* New York: Stein and Day, 1981; Richard S. Lukas, *Forgotten Holocaust: The Poles Under German Occupation 1939-1944.* Lexington: University Press of Kentucky, 1986; and Gabrielle Tyrnauer, "The Gypsy Awakening," *Reform Judaism,* 14:3 (Spring 1986), 6-8.

Incarnation of God in Christ.... In the new conception, God becomes man in a political sense as a member of the Aryan race whose highest representative on earth is the Fuhrer.[4]

As Tal sees the picture, this Nazi consciousness developed gradually in the decades following the First World War. Its roots reached back into the process of social secularization that was transforming the life of Germany. Its philosophic parents included the deists, the French encyclopedists, Feuerbach, the Young Hegelians and the evolutionists together with the new generation of scientists who through their escalating discoveries left the impression to many that a triumphant material civilization was about to dawn in Europe. In the end, Tal argues, "these intellectual and social movements struck a responsive chord in a rebellious generation, altered the traditional views of God, man, and society, and ultimately led to the pseudo-religious, pseudomessianic movement of Nazism."[5]

The principal theological problem posed by the Holocaust for contemporary morality is how to appropriate the sense of human liberation that lay at the heart of Nazi ideology. The Nazis were correct in at least one respect. They rightly perceived that some basic changes were underway in human consciousness. The impact of the new science and technology, with its underlying philosophy of freedom, was beginning to provide humankind on a mass scale with a Promethean-type experience of escape from prior bonds. People were starting to perceive, however simply, a more enhanced sense of dignity and autonomy than most of Western Christian theology had previously conceded. Traditional theological concepts that had shaped much of the Christian moral perspective, notions such as divine punishment, hell, the wrath of God, and divine providence, were losing some of the hold they exercised over moral decision-making since biblical times. Christian theology had tended to accentuate the omnipotence of God which in turn intensified the impotence of human person and the rather inconsequential role played by the human community in the governance of the earth. The Nazis were saying "no" to this previous relationship, trying literally to turn it on its head.

Michael Ryan has emphasized this direction of Nazism in his theological analysis of *Mein Kampf*. What is especially striking about Hitler's "salvation history," as Ryan terms it, is its willingness to confine itself in an absolute way to the limits of time:

---

4. "Forms of Pseudo-Religion in the German *Kulturbereich* Prior to the Holocaust," *Immanuel*, 3 (Winter 1973-74), 69.

5. *Christians and Jews in Germany*. Ithaca: Cornell University Press, 1975, 302-303.

It amounted to a resignation to the conditions of finitude, while at the same time asserting total power for itself within those conditions. This is what makes the logic of Mein Kampf theological. By asserting total control within the limits of finitude, Hitler deified himself and made himself into the Savior of the German people.[6]

Ryan insists that Hitler's worldview

amounted to the deliberate decision on the part of mass man to live within the limits of finitude without either the moral restraints or the hopes of traditional religion—in this case, Christianity.[7]

The challenge confronting theology after the Holocaust is to discover a way whereby the new sense of human freedom that is continuing to dawn might be affirmed but channelled into constructive rather than humanly destructive purposes. The understanding of the God-human person relationship must be significantly altered in light of the Holocaust. The intensified sense of power and human elevation that the Nazis recognized as a *novum* of our age needs to be acknowledged for what it is—a crucial and inescapable part of the process of human salvation. There is no turning back this changed divine-human relationship. That is why the mere repetition of biblical precepts, of the biblical view of God's relationship with his creation, will not suffice as a response to the Holocaust. Contemporary humanity finds itself in a "freer" situation relative to God than its biblical counterpart. People today perceive dimensions to the Genesis notion of co-creatorship which far exceed the consciousness of the biblical world.

As the moral philosopher Hans Jonas has reminded us, we are the first generation to face the responsibility of preserving the future of human and non-human life. No previous generation has had the possibilities for total destruction that lie before us. This theme has also been emphatically sounded in the American Catholic Bishops' Pastoral on Peace.[8]

The challenge before us then is whether post-Holocaust theology can articulate an understanding of God and religion which will prevent the newly rec-

---

6. "Hitler's Challenge to the Churches: A Theological-Political Analysis of *Mein Kampf*," in Franklin H. Littell and Hubert G. Locke (eds.), *The German Church Struggle and the Holocaust*. Detroit: Wayne State University Press, 160-161.

7. *Ibid.*

8. For the complete text of the Pastoral with commentary, cf. John T. Pawlikowski, OSM and Donald Senior, CP (eds.), *Biblical and Theological Reflections on* **The Challenge of Peace**. Wilmington: Michael Glazier, 1984. For a Catholic/Reform Jewish discussion of the Pastoral, cf. Annette Daum and Eugene Fisher (eds.), *The Challenge of Shalom for Catholics and Jews: A*

ognized creative power of humanity from being transformed into the destructive force unveiled in all its ugliness in the Shoah. Seen from the viewpoint of a social ethicist, the fundamental question before us is whether post-Holocaust humanity can discover a relationship with God which will morally ground the use of its vast new power to shape itself and the creation it has inherited. That is a fundamental issue that most Christian ethicists have skirted up till now.

Reflections on the divine-human relationship in light of the Holocaust have emerged in the last decade as one of the central theological discussions in Judaism. Unfortunately, as David Tracy has so rightly said, the same has not generally happened in Christian theology, especially among Catholics:

> ...the ultimate theological issue, the understanding of God, has yet to receive much reflection from Catholic theologians. And yet, as Schleiermacher correctly insisted, the doctrine of God can never be "another" doctrine for theology, but must pervade all doctrines. Here Jewish theology, in its reflections on the reality of God since the *Tremendum* of the Holocaust, has led the way for all serious theological reflection.[9]

Theological discussion about God in light of the Shoah has resulted in a variety of viewpoints among Jewish scholars. I cannot treat them in any comprehensive fashion in this presentation. Most Orthodox Jewish scholars have tended to downplay the Holocaust as a major turning point in our perception of the God-human person relationship. While they are acutely sensitive that the murder of six million innocent men, women and children has traumatized the Jewish people it is their belief that the event can still be incorporated into classical theological categories of evil. A few Reform Jewish scholars such as Eugene Borowitz have likewise de-emphasized the Holocaust as a theological issue in favor of the more traditional Reform Jewish concern with human autonomy.

One of the more prominent spokespersons for this point of view is Dr. David Hartman who will address us in a subsequent paper. In earlier writings and now in a major new book *A Living Covenant: The Innovative Spirit in Traditional Judaism*[10] he feels that contemporary renewal of traditional covenantal religion is the key to the survival of Judaism. Adopting a position

---

Dialogical Discussion Guide to the Catholic Bishops' Pastoral on Peace and War. Washington and New York: National Conference of Catholic Bishops and the Union of American Hebrew Congregations, 1985.

9. "Religious Values after the Holocaust: A Catholic View," in Abraham J. Peck (ed.), *Jews and Christians After the Holocaust.* Philadelphia: Fortress, 1982, 101.

10. New York: The Free Press, 1985.

similar to that advocated by the noted Christian ethicist James Gustafson about our inability to really know what God ultimately intends for humankind, Hartman stresses the development of new faithfulness to Torah observance as the only way of assuring communal survival and a measure of meaning in a frequently chaotic world. The Holocaust was certainly a part of this chaos which we will surely continue to remember. But in no way will it provide a basis for contemporary belief:

> Auschwitz, like all Jewish suffering of the past, must be absorbed and understood within the normative framework of Sinai. We will mourn forever because of the memory of Auschwitz. We will build a healthy new society because of the memory of Sinai.[11]

I stand in partial sympathy with Hartman and his colleagues. Even after the Holocaust our faith expression must be strongly rooted in the covenantal experience and promises. But I believe they have seriously underestimated the degree to which the Holocaust forces us to readjust some of our understanding of the biblical heritage. The Shoah is not merely the most gruesome and troubling example of the classical theological problem of evil. The classical categories of evil cannot handle it. To stop here in our reflections on the significance of the Holocaust for contemporary religious faith would threaten human survival. For we will fail to appreciate fully enough the magnitude of the power and consequent responsibility that has come into the hands of humanity. And failure on the part of humankind to recognize these new post-Holocaust realities may allow this power to once again pass into the hands of a new class of Nazis. The frontispiece to Alexander Donat's *The Holocaust Kingdom,* a quote from Revelation 6:8, poignantly reminds us of that continuing potential:

> And I looked, and beheld a pale horse and his name that sat on him was Death, and Hell followed with him. And power was given unto them over the fourth part of the earth, to kill with sword, and with hunger, and with death, and with the beasts of the earth.

Among those Jewish scholars who have argued for major theological reinterpretation of the God-human person relationship in light of the Shoah the names of Richard Rubenstein, Emil Fackenheim, Arthur Cohen and my distinguished colleague in this session Irving Greenberg stand out. I shall only

---

11. "New Jewish Religious Voice II: Auschwitz or Sinai," *The Ecumenist,* 21:1 (November/December 1982), 8.

briefly mention the perspectives of the first three with a somewhat more detailed analysis of Greenberg's approach in the hope of stimulating some constructive dialogue between us.

Rubenstein's volume *After Auschwitz*[12] caused a great stir in Jewish circles when it first appeared. Its boldly stated claim that the Shoah had buried any possibility of continued belief in a covenantal God of history and that in place of traditional faith we must now turn to a creed of "paganism" which defines human existence as wholly and totally an earthly existence shook the foundation of Judaism. When the dust had somewhat settled the prevailing opinion was that Rubenstein had gone much too far. But even many who reject his "paganism" verdict, such as Steven Katz, consider him "absolutely correct" in his judgment that classical categories of evil simply do not work relative to the God-human person relationship when confronted by the Shoah[13]

Fackenheim, Cohen and Greenberg, in their approach to the post-Holocaust divine reality, stop far short of Rubenstein's total rejection of a covenantal God. But despite some significant differences among them, they speak with unified voice regarding the need for a major restatement of this relationship in light of the Shoah.

In his many writings, but especially in the volume *The Jewish Return into History*[14] Emil Fackenheim states his conviction that the image of God was destroyed during the Shoah. Our task today, a mandate incumbent in a special way upon the survivors of the Holocaust, is to restore the divine image, but one that conveys a sense of a new curtailment of God's power in comparison with past images. Arthur Cohen picks up this same theme, but uses more philosophically-oriented language to make his point. In *The Tremendum: A Theological Interpretation of the Holocaust*[15] Cohen pointedly rejects the continued viability of any image of God as the strategist of human history. A post-Shoah God can legitimately be perceived (and must be so perceived if radical evil is to remain in check) as

> the mystery of our futurity, always our *posse* never our acts. If we can begin to see God less as an interferer whose insertion is welcome (when it accords with our needs) and more as the immensity whose reality is our prefiguration, whose speech and silence are metaphors for our language and distortion, whose plenitude and unfolding are the hope of our futurity, we shall have won a sense of

---

12. Indianapolis: Bobbs-Merrill, 1966. Also cf. "Some Perspectives on Religious Faith After Auschwitz," in Littell and Locke (eds.), *The German Church Struggle*, 256-268.

13. Cf. *Post-Holocaust Dialogues: Critical Studies in Modern Jewish Thought*. New York: New York University Press, 1983, 176.

14. New York: Schocken Books, 1978.

15. New York: Crossroad, 1981.

God whom we may love and honor, but whom we no longer fear and from whom we no longer demand.[16]

Turning now to Irving Greenberg, we find that his language about the effects of the Holocaust on the divine image are not as blunt as those of Fackenheim's, but he shares the conviction that a major readjustment is required of our statement of the force of the covenantal obligations upon humanity in light of the Shoah. "The Nazis," he says, "unleashed all-out violence against the covenant...." Their program for the Final Solution involved a total assault on Jewish life and values. For Greenberg, "the degree of success of this attack constitutes a fundamental contradiction to the covenant of life and redemption."[17]

The reality of the Nazi fury forces a thorough reconsideration of the nature of moral obligation upon the contemporary Jewish community and seemingly by implication upon all those other believers (Christians and Muslims) who in some way regard the Sinai covenant as foundational for their faith expression. For this covenant has called Jews as witnesses to the world for God and for a final perfection. "In light of the Holocaust," insists Greenberg, "it is obvious that this role opened the Jews to a murderous fury from which there was no escape. Yet the Divine could not or would not save them from this fate. Therefore, morally speaking, God must repent of the covenant, i.e., do *teshuvah* for having given his chosen people a task that was unbearably cruel and dangerous without having provided for their protection. Morally speaking, then, God can have no claims on the Jews by dint of the covenant."[18]

The end result of any serious reflection on the Sinai Covenant in light of the Holocaust experience, as Greenberg sees it, is simply the disappearance of any "commanded" dimension on the part of God. "Covenantally speaking, one cannot *order* another to step forward to die."[19] Any understanding of covenantal obligation must now be voluntary:

> One cannot *order* another to go on a suicide mission. Out of shared values, one can only ask for volunteers.... No divine punishment can enforce the covenant, for there is no risked punishment so terrible that it can match the punishment risked by continuing faithfulness to the covenant.[20]

---

16. *The Tremendum*, 97.

17. "The Voluntary Covenant," *Perspectives* #3. New York: National Jewish Resource Center, 1982, 14.

18. *Ibid.* 15

19. *Ibid.*

20. *Ibid.* 16.

The voluntary nature of the post-Holocaust covenantal relationship unquestionably heightens human responsibility in the eyes of Greenberg:

> If after the Temple's destruction, Israel moved from junior participant to true partner in the covenant, then after the Holocaust, the Jewish people is called upon to become the senior partner in action. In effect, God was saying to humans: you stop the Holocaust. You bring the redemption. You act to ensure that it will never again occur. I will be with you totally in whatever happens, but you must do it.[21]

My basic response to the post-Holocaust reflections of Fackenheim, Cohen and especially Greenberg is that, despite some reservations, they provide the basic parameters within which we need to understand the God-human person relationship today and its connections with the foundations for contemporary morality. For one, consciousness of the role of the human community in preserving human history from further eruptions of radical evil akin to Nazism has been greatly enhanced, as all three have rightly insisted. Humanity finds itself after the Holocaust facing the realization that "future" is no longer something God will guarantee. Survival, whether for the people of Israel or humanity at large, is now more than ever a human proposition. In their differing ways Fackenheim, Cohen and Greenberg have made this fact abundantly clear. And we need to be profoundly grateful for that. They have clearly confronted us with the post-Holocaust reality that any simplistic belief in an interventionist God of history was buried in the ashes of the Shoah. Stopping massive human destruction is now far more evidently than before a burden primarily incumbent upon us. We must learn to save ourselves from future instances of holocaust, nuclear or otherwise. We are called to give a "right now" answer to D.H. Lawrence's cry, "God of Justice, when wilt Thou teach them to save themselves?"[22] We no longer have the luxury, in fact it would be the height of human irresponsibility after the Holocaust, to imagine that God will do it in response to simple petitions of prayer. Perhaps because of the freedom God has granted humanity he cannot do it. I might add here that as part of our search for a meaningful notion of God after the Shoah, one that would heighten our role in human salvation, we may need to explore such traditional sources as the notion of divine self-constriction in the act of creation that is present in Jewish mystical literature.

But despite my gratitude to Fackenheim, Cohen and Greenberg I must demur a bit from their approach. Have they left us *too* much on our own? Does

---

21. *Ibid.* 17-18.
22. *Selected Poems.* London: Penguin Books, 1967, 144.

God have any significant role after the Holocaust experience in the development of a moral ethos within humanity that can keep radical evil in check? I do not believe any of the Jewish writers have adequately dealt with this question. The role they have assigned to God is not potent enough in my judgment.

The post-Holocaust theological vision must be one that recognizes both the new creative possibilities inherent in the human condition as well as the utter necessity that this creative potential be influenced by a genuine encounter with the living and judging God. Only such an encounter will direct the use of this creative potential away from the destruction represented by Nazism. We need to find a way of articulating a notion of a transcendent God which can counterbalance the potential for evil that remains very much a live possibility in the contemporary human situation. In other words we shall have to recover a fresh sense of transcendence to accompany our heightened sense of human responsibility after the Shoah. This is something I do not find Fackenheim, Cohen and Greenberg addressing as yet in a persuasive way. Men and women will once more need to experience contact with a personal power beyond themselves, a power that heals the destructive tendencies still lurking within humanity. The newly liberated person, to be able to work consistently for the creation of a just and sustainable society, must begin to sense that there exists a judgment upon human endeavors that goes beyond mere human judgment. Such a sense of judgment is missing in Fackenheim's emphasis on human restoration of the divine image, in Cohen's language about God as our "posse," and in Greenberg's notion of the voluntary covenant, as valid as each notion is in itself.

The Holocaust has shattered all simplistic notions of a "commanding God." On this point I go full way with Fackenheim, Cohen and Greenberg. Such a "commanding" God can no longer be the touchstone of ethical behavior. But the Shoah has also exposed humanity's desperate need to restore a relationship with a "compelling" God, *compelling* because we have experienced through symbolic encounter with this God a healing, a strengthening, an affirming that buries any need to assert our humanity through the destructive, even deadly, use of human power. This sense of a compelling Parent God who has gifted humanity, whose vulnerability for the Christian has been shown in the Cross, is the meaningful foundation for an adequate moral ethos after the Holocaust. Hence I part company to a significant extent with Cohen, Fackenheim and Greenberg in positing this "compelling" God. I believe their approach leaves God's role too indirect. Talk of a purely voluntary covenant, of human restoration of the divine image or of God as simply the "posse" of the human future leaves us in the final analysis with an overly impotent God. Some have suggested to me that "compelling" may be too strong a replacement for "commanding" in speaking about the post-Holocaust God. Perhaps they are right;

perhaps I have tipped the scales too much back toward a pre-Holocaust vision of God. These critics have offered the alternative of speaking about a "God to whom we are drawn" which admittedly is more cumbersome than "compelling." This inherent and perduring "drawing" power of God would substitute for pre-Holocaust models which emphasized God's "imposition" upon humanity.

I am still inclined at this point to stay with the "compelling" vocabulary. But whatever image eventually wins the day the basic point must be made that post-Shoah humanity needs to rediscover a permanent relationship with God who remains a direct source of strength and influence in the conduct of human affairs.

In speaking of the need to rediscover a "compelling" God I believe I am close to the stage Elie Wiesel has reached as he has probed the depth of this event these many years. Despite the remaining ambiguities, despite the apparent divine failures in covenantal responsibility, atheism is not the answer for contemporary humanity. After we have exhausted ourselves in protesting against God's non-intervention during the Holocaust, we still cannot let God go away permanently. Any attempt, Wiesel insists, to make the Holocaust "fit" into a divine plan, any belief that somehow we can imagine a universe congruent with it, renders God a moral monster and the universe a nightmare beyond endurance. But, as Robert McAfee Brown, has put it,

> ...for Wiesel and for many others the issue will not go away. He must *contest* with God, concerning the moral outrage that somehow seems to be within the divine plan. How can one affirm a God whose "divine plan" could include such barbarity? For Wiesel, the true "contemporary" is not the modern skeptic, but the ancient Job, the one who dares to ask questions of God, even though Wiesel feels that Job gave in a little too quickly at the end.[23]

Wiesel hints that after all is said and done the Holocaust may reveal that divine and human liberation are very much intertwined and that, despite continuing tension, both God and humanity yearn for each other as a result. As a result of this linkage, Wiesel is prepared to say that human acts of justice and compassion help to liberate God, to restore the divine image as Fackenheim has put it. Job, says Wiesel, "did not suffer in vain; thanks to him, we know that it is given to man to transform divine injustice into human justice and compassion."[24] But they also show the need for God's continuing presence, for the human person who claims total freedom from God will not likely pursue

---

23. "The Holocaust as a Problem in Moral Choice," in Harry Cargas (ed.), *When God and Man Failed: Non-Jewish Views of the Holocaust*. New York: Macmillan, 1981, 94.

24. *Messengers of God*. New York: Random House, 1976, 235.

such a ministry of justice and compassion for very long. so the human person is also liberated from the corrupting desire to cut all ties to the Creator. At this point we must ask the inevitable question. How can this "compelling God" of whom I speak be discovered in our time as the ground of contemporary morality? Strange as it may seem, the Holocaust provides us with some help in answering this question. For if the Shoah reveals one permanent quality of human life, it is the enduring presence of, the enduring human need for, symbolic affirmation and communication. What Reinhold Niebuhr called the vitalistic side of humanity has not been permanently obliterated. But increasingly in the west it has been relegated almost exclusively to the realm of play and recreation. The Enlightenment and its aftermath caused a bifurcation in humanity which resulted in reason being elevated to overwhelming dominance in the self-definition of the person. All other human dimensions were relegated to an inferior status. Ethics became far too rational a discipline and far too dominated by the scientific mentality. The liberals in Germany were powerless in fighting Nazism because they had adopted such a model. The Nazis were far more perceptive in recognizing the centrality of the vitalistic in human life.

It is my judgment then that *recovery* of an abiding contact with the personal Creator God first revealed in the Hebrew Scriptures is as indispensable a starting point for social ethics today as recognition of our enhanced co-creational responsibilities for the world. The two go hand-in-hand. Any attempt to construct a social ethic for the post-Holocaust world by merely *assuming* the continued reality of this divine presence or by turning merely to natural law, Kantian rational consistency or psychoanalysis for grounding will not work. The kind of post-Shoah relationship between God and humanity which I take as pivotal for social morality in our time will come only through liturgical encounter primarily and secondarily through personal prayer. The failure of nearly all contemporary social ethics to deal constructively with the role of symbols in society, especially liturgical symbolism, and with prayer and to recognize how crucial they are for overcoming the prevailing one-dimensionality infecting western society has left us with an increasingly barren public morality.

We may not need to return to the tradition of medieval morality plays. But we desperately need to understand that without liturgy and prayer there is no real way of overcoming self-centeredness and the destructive use of power evidenced in the Holocaust save for the kind of spiritless centralization of authority suggested by Robert Heilbroner in his *An Inquiry into the Human Prospect*.[25] Psychoanalysis can uncover humanity's neuroses. But by itself it

25. New York: W.W. Norton, 1980.

cannot fully heal. Sacramental celebration and prayer are crucial to this end. *God is a Person* experienced through symbolic encounter. This revolutionary revelation of the Hebrew Scriptures and the New Testament remains a touchstone of a sound social ethic for our society.

Much more could be said about the God-problem in light of the Holocaust. But in the interest of briefly addressing several other crucial issues I shall end my discussion of it at this point. The three remaining topics that I should like to consider within the context of a reflection on the Holocaust experience are (1) Christology, (2) a theology of religious pluralism, and (3) the morality of power in our time.

In the two decades since Vatican Council II issued its historic declaration on the Church and the Jewish people in its document *Nostra Aetate* considerable progress has been made, even in official ecclesiastical statements, on the constructive restatement of the theological relationship between Christianity and the people Israel. Individual theologians in both Europe and America have led the way. Paul Van Buren, Franz Mussner, Clemens Thoma, A. Roy Eckardt and others have made extremely important contributions in this regard. My own work *Christ in the Light of the Christian-Jewish Dialogue* is a modest attempt to survey theological developments and propose the outlines of a new theological model.[26] And official statements from major Catholic and Protestant bodies, and from individual Christian leaders including the present Pope, John Paul II, have increasingly stressed the deep bonding from a theological and a spiritual point of view that continues to exist between Judaism and Christianity. There is no other religion with which the Church shares such an intimate bond. More and more, many official statements such as the new Vatican *Notes*, the World Council of Churches Study document and the statement of the Rheinland synod[27] seem to be pushing us in the direction of a notion of a shared covenantal tradition. Drawing upon an earlier statement of Pope John Paul II, the Vatican *Notes*, for example, described Judaism and Christianity as "linked together at the very level of their identity" (1:2).

As one who has worked on the theological dimensions of the Christian-Jewish relationship for well over a decade I certainly identify with the basic spirit and thrust of these statements as they try to restore Christian faith expression to its original Jewish context. Its loss has frequently proven disastrous over the centuries not only for the safety and even survival of the Jewish people but

---

26. New York/Ramsey: Paulist/Stimulus, 1982.

27. For the complete text of these documents, cf. Helga Croner (ed.), *More Stepping Stones to Jewish-Christian Relations.* New York/Mahwah: Paulist/Stimulus, 1985. For earlier statements, cf. Helga Croner (ed.), *Stepping Stones to Further Jewish-Christian Relations.* London/New York: Stimulus Books, 1977.

for the overall moral outlook and commitment of the Church as Rosemary Ruether, Friedrich Heer and A. Roy Eckhardt have correctly told us.

The seeming movement in many of these documents toward a single covenantal model for the Jewish-Christian relationship, rather than the double covenantal perspective which I endorse along with Franz Mussner and some others, is something that I feel, however, needs considerable discussion. I raise it here, even though it is not possible to pursue the question, lest in our enthusiasm for the important new directions in these documents that both single and double covenantal theologians can legitimately endorse we settle an issue without working through all its many implications. Can I as a Christian, for example, claim to fully share in the one covenant with the people Israel when I have not truly experienced that people's pain and trauma in the last two millennia? And is a single covenantal model, no matter how positively stated with respect to Judaism's ongoing validity, still in great danger of ultimately positing an absorption of Judaism? I recognize there are also problems with the double covenant model, and I must confess that there are times I have been tempted to accept the invitation of Paul Van Buren and others and shift over to a single covenantal viewpoint. But in my judgment this issue is far from resolution, and many questions, including the two I just raised, have not been sufficiently answered or even probed for that matter.

Space will not allow us to consider the various proposals offered thus far for a renewed theology of the Christian-Jewish relationship. There is little consensus as yet among those who have addressed themselves to the question. But there are some common agreements about certain directions which are worthy of note. These are: (1) that the Christ Event did not invalidate the Jewish faith perspective; (2) that Christianity is not superior to Judaism, nor is it the fulfillment of Judaism as previously maintained; (3) that the Sinai covenant is in principle as crucial to Christian faith expression as the covenant in Christ; and (4) that Christianity needs to reincorporate dimensions from its original Jewish context.

As for general areas that still need further attention I would point to the following as pivotal. The first is the need to relate the discussion about the theology of the Christian-Jewish relationship and its implications for Christology to the discussion of what David Tracy has correctly argued is the more fundamental God-problem after the Shoah. So far few of the Christian theologians who have turned their attention creatively to the theology of Christian-Jewish relations have in any way linked it to theological reflection on the Holocaust. I have tried to begin this process myself,[28] but I would be

___

28. Cf. *Christ in the Light*, 136-147. Also cf. "The Holocaust and Contemporary

the first to grant that my effort remains incomplete. David Tracy has not really pursued the issue in any detail, except with respect to the question of theological methodology about which I will say more shortly. Jurgen Moltmann has offered some promising possibilities on the relationship between Christology and the God-problem after the Holocaust, but he has not really thought through the specific implications for the theology of the Christian-Jewish relationship.[29]

Johannes Metz has begun to examine the implications of the Holocaust for Christian theology. In a contribution to the *Concilium* series' volume on the Holocaust he proposes three theses as indispensable for theological reflection by the Church in light of the Shoah: (1) "Christian theology after Auschwitz must—at long last—be guided by the insight that Christians can form and sufficiently understand their identity only in the face of "the Jews" (2) "Because of Auschwitz the statement 'Christians can only form and appropriately understand their identity in the face of "the Jews"' has been sharpened as follows: 'Christians can protect their identity only in front of and together with the history of the beliefs of the Jews'"; " (3) "Christian theology after Auschwitz must stress anew the Jewish dimension in Christian beliefs and must overcome the forced blocking-out of the Jewish heritage within Christianity."[30] Certainly Metz is moving in the right direction in his strong advocacy of these three theses. However, he still needs to apply them much more specifically and in much greater detail to an exposition of the meaning of God and Christ for the contemporary Christian than he has done to date.

These three theses build upon some previous reflections by Metz where he firmly argued that any statement made by Christian theology in our day, any attempt to find meaning for life after the Shoah, must be considered "blasphemy" if it does not meet the test of this *historical* event. Metz here opens to us another area of significance for Christian theology in terms of the Holocaust. It is the consequences of the Holocaust for basic methodology in the process of theological construction. Metz insists, and quite correctly I might add, that theology after the Holocaust must make the experience of history central to its formulations. All Christian theology must be rooted in historical con-

---

Christology," in Elisabeth Schussler - Fiorenza and David Tracy (eds.), *The Holocaust as Interruption. Concilium* (October 1984). Edinburgh: T & T Clark, 1984, 43-52.

29. Cf. *The Crucified God.* New York: Harper & Row, 1974. For a critique of Moltmann, cf. A. Roy Eckardt, "Christians and Jews: Along a Theological Frontier," *Encounter,* 40:2 (Spring 1979)), 97-110.

30. Cf. "Facing the Jews. Christian Theology After Auschwitz," in Schussler-Fiorenza and Tracy (eds.), *The Holocaust,* 26, 28, and 31.

sciousness after the Shoah and in the realization that salvation can be achieved only in alliance with Jews within history:

> But this means that we Christians for our own sakes are from now on assigned to the victims of Auschwitz—assigned, in fact, in an alliance belonging to the heart of *saving history*, provided the word "history" in this Christian expression is to have a definite meaning and not just serve as a screen for a triumphalist metaphysic of salvation which never learns from catastrophes nor finds in them a cause for conversion....[31]

David Tracy has pursued the methodological implications of the Holocaust for Christian theology with greater vigor then Metz. He too focuses on the need for Christians to begin to take seriously concrete historical events like the Holocaust and the emergence of the State of Israel. This can no longer be avoided. Neither a purely metaphysical approach to theology nor merely an emphasis on historical consciousness in the abstract will do after Auschwitz.[32] Tracy praises the liberation theologians for having begun to treat history with the seriousness it deserves, though he faults them for not relating their thought to the Holocaust experience.

At this point it is necessary for me to diverge for a moment and address a problem that has troubled many of us in the Christian-Jewish dialogue. It has surfaced as a deep concern within the Christian Study Group on Judaism and the Jewish People sponsored by the National Conference of Christians and Jews. I speak of what appears to us as a return to a sometimes blatant form of anti-Judaism in liberation theology that seems to totally ignore *Nostra Aetate* and the subsequent official Catholic and Protestant statements. My colleague Clark Williamson[33] and I have both investigated this disturbing trend. Not all liberation theologians are guilty of it. In fact, Gustavo Gutierrez and Jose Miguez Bonino make a positive contribution in my judgment by returning us to the Exodus God of history as a central, *ongoing* source of revelation for Christian faith in our time. But with Leonardo Boff, Jon Sobrino and J. Severino Croatto we face an overwhelmingly, displacement-oriented theology of Judaism which can no longer go unchallenged despite the real contribu-

---

31. *The Emergent Church.* New York: Crossroad, 1981, 19-20.

32. "The Interpretation for Theological Texts After the Holocaust," Unpublished Lecture, International Conference on the Holocaust, Indiana University, Bloomington, IN, Fall 1982, 16-17.

33. Cf. *Christ in the Light,* 59-73. Also, cf. Clark Williamson, "Christ Against the Jews: A Review of Jon Sobrino's Christology," *Encounter,* 40 (Fall 1979), 403-412 and "Old Wine in New Skins? A Critique of Modern Christology." Paper presented to the Christian Study Group on Judaism and the Jewish People, Cathedral College, Douglaston, New York, 4 October 1985.

tions these theologians have made to the overall life of the Church, especially in Latin America. We all have blind spots. And I am afraid their weakness here is very glaring to anyone who has integrated the directions mandated by recent Church statements. I would hope that Orbis Books which has performed a real service in bringing many of these writings to the English-speaking world might take some constructive editorial responsibility in future works or new editions of existing volumes regarding this situation. In so doing it would be paying tribute to its founder the late Philip Scharper who was one of the early pioneers in confronting the Church's negative theology of Judaism.

Before leaving the issue of the "return to history" as a central methodological focus in post-Holocaust Christian theology let me interject an issue that moves more into the realm of ethics. What I have in mind is the role that power is to play in the new historical consciousness to which Metz, Tracy, Fackenheim and Greenberg have called us in light of the Shoah. Greenberg has probably been the most direct in positing the relationship between power and the Holocaust experience. "Power inescapably corrupts," he writes, "but its assumption is inescapable" after Shoah.

In Greenberg's perspective it would be immoral to abandon the quest for power post-Auschwitz. The only option open to us today, if we are to avoid further repetitions of the human degradation and evil of the Nazi period, is to combine the assumption of power with what Greenberg calls the creation of "better mechanisms of self-criticism, correction and repentance." Only in this way can we utilize power "without being the unwitting slaves of bloodshed or an exploitative status quo."[34]

I share Greenberg's conviction that a central implication of the return to history demanded by the Holocaust is the willingness to use power. Thus, for me, a meaningful Christian ethic cannot simply reject the use of power in principle, though it certainly may decide that certain configurations of power (e.g. nuclear weaponry) are totally immoral even when the threat of human survival looms large. Nonetheless, those of us engaged in post-Holocaust reflection on theology and ethics need to probe this question more deeply. Our context for doing so must be the prophetic warning issued by the Catholic philosopher Romano Guardini soon after the Nazi experience:

> In the coming epoch, the essential problem will no longer be that of increasing power—though power will continue to increase at an even swifter tempo—but of curbing it. The core of the epoch's intellectual task will be to integrate power

---

34. "The Third Great Cycle in Jewish History," *Perspectives*. New York: National Jewish Resource Center, 1981, 24-25.

into life in such a way that man can employ power without forfeiting his humanity, or to surrender his humanity to power and perish.[35]

Continuing on now with our discussion of theological methodology in light of the Christian-Jewish dialogue, several other key points need raising. First of all, as Dr. Eugene Fisher has correctly said, Christian tradition will have little positive value for the construction of a contemporary theology of the Jewish-Christian relationship. This was implicitly acknowledged at Vatican Council II, as Dr. Fisher has noted. Of all the conciliar documents *Nostra Aetate* is the only one which is devoid of references to the tradition of the Church.[36] As for Sacred Scripture as a resource, we have a bit more to draw on. Certainly, the reflections of the mature Paul at the end of his pastoral ministry in Romans 9-11 affirm the continuing validity of the Jewish covenant and undercut any simple displacement theology. Improved exegesis can also help moderate some of the supposed opposition between Jesus and the Pharisees and Jesus and Torah. But I believe we must candidly admit that the New Testament, especially in books such as John, Hebrews and Acts, leaves us with some genuine problems for a new constructive theology of Judaism from a Christian perspective. I remain firmly convinced that unless we are willing to embrace a theological hermeneutic that allows for some notion of ongoing revelation in the Church we shall not get very far in our efforts at rethinking the Christian-Jewish relationship theologically. At best we might be able to reach the "mystery" theology of Romans, but that to my mind remains far from adequate.

Looking at the methological question from a somewhat different perspective we also need to recognize as Christians that documents such as the 1985 *Notes* have now made the inclusion of biblical and post-biblical Jewish reflections an indispensable resource for all Christian theological reflection. These reflections must now be seen by Christian scholars as obligatory data for their own expositions of the Christian message. There is no authentic and complete proclamation of the gospel which does not integrate Jewish insights. Hence, as Gabriel Moran has recently observed, what we are doing in the Christian-Jewish dialogue is not simply creating a Christian theology of the Jewish people for use when we happen to encounter Jews in interreligious conversation, but transforming the very structure and expression of the totality of Christian faith proclamation which for so very long has been predi-

---

35. *Power and Responsibility*. Chicago: Henry Regnery, 1961, XIII.

36. Cf. "The Evolution of a Tradition: From *Nostra Aetate* to the *'Notes,'" Christian-Jewish Relations,* 18:4 (December 1985), 33.

cated on the superiority and opposition of Christianity to Judaism in fundamental ways.[37]

Most of this presentation has focused on concerns that I have regarding
Christianity's continuing response to the dialogue with the Jewish people. A
word is in order now, however, about the implications of the Christian
rethinking process for Jews. To be sure the specifics of the response are primarily the responsibility of Jewish scholars. But insofar as Jews laud the new
theology of partnership and bonding that has begun to appear, even in official
ecclesiastical declarations, then I believe that in principle they have a con-
comitant obligation to ask what such a theology means for their theological
understanding of Christianity and their use of Christian religious insights.
Jews cannot cheer for this emerging Christian theology if they fail to confront
its implications for Jewish faith expression.

To this end, I welcome those constructive attempts at developing a model
for the Jewish-Christian relationship from the Jewish point of view. I shall
here only refer to one present proposal, that advanced by my plenary colleague Irving Greenberg in some of his writings.[38]

Greenberg now sees Christianity and Judaism as authentic outgrowths of
the biblical covenant. Christian faith, which Greenberg describes as operating
fundamentally within a "sacramental mode," is closer in many ways than
post-biblical Judaism to the original biblical tradition. Even the central
Christian notion of the Incarnation, the basis of the Church's sacramental
approach to faith expression, ultimately operates within classical biblical
modes even if from the perspective of the Hebrew Scriptures it violates certain biblical principles. It still focuses on the need to achieve redemption and
to narrow the gap between the divine and human, a narrowing which requires
divine initiative through miracles. Such an approach may have a genuine
value for the Gentiles for whom it is basically intended and does serve to
grant Christianity legitimate roots in the convenantal tradition of the Bible.
But it does lock Christian faith expression into a mode that Greenberg seems
to feel will make it difficult for the Church to really accept the new burdens
incumbent upon humanity in light of the Holocaust experience.

Judaism, however, though it was also once in the biblical mode, moved
beyond this beginning with the rabbinic period. While the Christians were
developing their "new" covenant, Jews were renewing their covenant in a

---

37. "A More Radical Approach Still Needed," *The Alternative,* 12:2 (1985) 4-8.
38. "The Relationship of Judaism and Christianity: Towards a New Organic Model,"
Quarterly Review, 4:4 (Winter 1984), 4-22. Also cf. his essay in Eugene Fisher, A. James Rudin
and Marc Tanenbaum (eds.), *Twenty Years of Jewish-Catholic Relations.* New York/Mahwah:
Paulist, 1986.

major way. In this new post-biblical stage of Jewish faith expression God becomes more hidden and Jews assume a more worldly stance. This stage represents a significant maturation of the God-humankind relationship in which men and women acquire an unprecedented share of responsibility for creation. Greenberg definitely considers this form of religion the more advanced form of religion, a form that the Gentiles may not yet be ready to assume.

Greenberg also confesses that he has advanced this model with some apprehension. His contention that Christianity stands closer today to biblical covenantal religion than Judaism may feed traditional Christian triumphalism and supersessionism with no guarantee that enough Christians will make the effort to rethink this tradition. On balance, however, he feels the risk worth taking because of his experiences in the dialogue thus far.

I, for one, am glad that Greenberg has taken the risk of suggesting this new model. I think it can make for some intriguing discussions. While I am unable to offer a thorough critique of it here, I must say I find it inadequate in many respects even though I can identify very much with Greenberg's understanding of what post-biblical religion is all about and that it is the mode of faith expression basically demanded by the experience of the Holocaust. My main point of disagreement would be his claim that the Incarnation locks Christianity into a biblical mode of faith expression. If one takes seriously some of the explorations of the meaning of the Incarnation offered by Jurgen Moltmann and by Pope John Paul II in his encyclical *Laborem Exercens,* I think a case can be made that the Incarnational mode is much closer to the rabbinic mode than Greenberg seems to allow. Also, the way Greenberg has stated the relationship in this model, there seems little that Judaism can gain by way of spiritual enrichment from its encounter with Christianity. Yet in earlier writings Greenberg argued that recovery of the sacramental was precisely one of the benefits that Judaism might gain from the dialogue. But now the sacramental mode seems outdated and without any inherent value for Judaism. Is Greenberg now repudiating what he argued in previous writings? And if so, are there now no areas where Jewish faith expression might possibly be enhanced through interaction with Christianity?

One last comment on this discussion. I think it points up the need for an ongoing vehicle, the equivalent of the bilaterals that have been part of inter-Christian ecumenism, in the Christian-Jewish dialogue. Such a bilateral would be the ideal place for in-depth discussion of the model Greenberg has offered us and would help generate other models. I sincerely hope we may see the establishment of some such bilateral in the near future.

In addition to serious reflection by individual Jewish scholars on the implications for Jewish faith expression of the new theological models being

proposed by Christian scholars for the Christian-Jewish relationship, I am
convinced the time has also come for Jewish leaders to try to develop a consensus statement on whether Christianity in any way represents a covenantal
moment from the Jewish faith perspective. I think it is vital for Jews to have
some concrete experience in writing a consensus document of this kind so
that there might be better appreciation of the difficulties involved when any
official Christian body attempts it. Also, Jews cannot continue critiquing the
Church's theological approach to Judaism without an equal opportunity for
Christians to do the same with a Jewish statement.

To close off my presentation, I would like to turn my attention to an issue
that Rabbi A. James Rudin of the American Jewish Committee perceptively
raised in a luncheon address at the national workshop in St. Louis. Rudin
claimed that no religious tradition will be truly safe from discrimination or
persecution until we all develop a positive theology of religious pluralism
that goes beyond mere toleration. I think he is quite right.

Two well-known Jewish scholars in the dialogue, David Hartman and
Shemaryahu Talmon, offered us somewhat contrasting, even clashing, models for such a theology a number of years ago. They bear a second look.

Hartman maintained that an exaggerated stress on *truth* has been the chief
cause of interreligious conflict in the past. Truth, he argues, does not serve as
the primary religious category for Judaism. He calls for a new pluralistic spirituality anchored in a radical, all-embracing abandonment of previous claims
to truth on the part of Judaism, Christianity and Islam. He rejects any "inter-
mediate" position which views commitment to pluralism as a temporary position by a religious group until it experiences final confirmation of its faith
perspective in the eschatological era. He writes:

> We cannot in some way leap to some eschaton and live in two dimensions; to
> be pluralistic now but to be monistic in our eschatological vision is bad faith.
> We have to recognize that ultimately spiritual monism is a disease. It leads to
> the type of spiritual arrogance that has brought bloodshed to history. Therefore
> we have to rethink our eschatology, and rethink the notion of multiple spiritual
> communities and their relationship to a monotheistic faith.[39]

Talmon's proposal was originally presented to a multilateral dialogue
sponsored by the World Council of Churches.[40] He put forth two central principles for a theology of religious pluralism. The first is that such a theology

---

39. "Jews and Christians in the World of Tomorrow," *Immanuel* 6 (Spring 1976), 79.

40. "Towards World Community: Resources for Living Together—A Jewish View," *The
Ecumenical Review* 26 (October 1974), 617.

must draw upon the particularistic resources of each faith community. He rejects any approach that would try its formulation by finding common bases among all religious traditions. Talmon's second principle stands in direct opposition to Hartman's viewpoint. We need to acknowledge, he says, that most religious traditions harbor in varying degrees dreams of universal acceptance by force or persuasion. Judaism is no exception to the rule. The question then is how can the various faiths produce a theology of religious pluralism if each really desires universal acknowledgement of its particular spiritual truth. The answer, Talmon suggests, lies in the growth of a common mentality. Having laid their respective eschatological goals on the table, each faith community will agree to look upon the task of building world community as fundamentally non-eschatological or, at best, pre-eschatological. This involves the clear resolve that the process of building global interdependence must never become the occasion for activist eschatological realization and for the proselytization that it implies. Talmon thus does not demand the abandonment of eschatological truth claims as a pre-condition for the development of authentic religious pluralism in the manner of Hartman.

My personal sympathy is far more with Hartman than with Talmon. There must be some modification of eschatological truth claims for a genuine theology of religious pluralism. But I do agree somewhat with Talmon on one point. Such a theology cannot be built simply on universal elements in our respective faith traditions. It must grow out of our particularistic features as well.

A theology of religious pluralism might allow us to say we have more than others but never could it permit us to say we have a hold on all significant religious insight. This does not mean that each religious tradition is incapable of providing salvation for its adherents. What we need to recognize is that all of us are saved in our incompleteness. Along with Paul Tillich I believe a theology of religious pluralism requires some notion of an ongoing revelatory process.[41] I also acknowledge with Tillich that there may be a central event or events in the history of revelation. But "central" in my judgment need not imply exclusivity. As a Christian I would at least posit *both* Sinai and the Easter event as equally central, and I would be open to a possible expansion of the list. Also, calling a revelatory event central does not in my mind automatically connote "completeness." A central event need not make all other revelatory experiences secondary and by implication of lesser value. But this has been precisely the problem with the way Christianity has usually presented its notion of the centrality of the Christ Event. I would still hold to the cen-

---

41. *The Future of Religions,* ed. by Jerald C. Brauer. New York: Harper & Row, 1966, 81.

trality of the Christ Event, but the understanding of such centrality requires modification. Constructing a positive theology of religious pluralism, let me emphasize, is still very much in its infancy. Because it will have to deal with core elements of our faith traditions it cannot be done quickly and haphazardly. But with Rabbi Rudin I share the conviction it is something that deserves our serious attention.

As we go about this task on a theological level, let us not lose sight nonetheless of some particular consequences. As we approach another set of national elections in this country over the next several years I would summon all religious groups in this land to a rededication to the spirit of religious pluralism which has basically served us well in this nation. As a Catholic I would especially urge my own church to give faithful witness to the principles enunciated in Vatican Council II's *Declaration on Religious Liberty* which in so many ways is a product of the American Catholic experience. I am not suggesting that we do not need some new reflection on the meaning of religion's role in the public life and culture of this republic because I sincerely believe we do. But let us never lose sight of our precious legacy of religious pluralism as we engage in that reflection.

In this connection I would especially like to commend Msgr. George Higgins who has been a source of inspiration to so many of us in the dialogue for his forthright condemnation of the attack in 1985 upon the American Jewish Congress, and by implication all American Jews, by the late Fr. Virgil Blum, of the Catholic League for Religious and Civil Rights. Fr. Blum argued that the American Jewish Congress has been responsible for the destructive secularization of American society through its lawsuits in support of religious liberty. Neither Msgr. Higgins nor I would completely agree with Congress' approach to the First Amendment in all respects. That, however, is not the core issue. Msgr. Higgins stated it well in his YARDSTICK column of October 14, 1985:

> ...both Jews and Catholics have the right in our society to file these briefs and to submit their views to the public forum.... Father Blum's real problem...stems from his truncated notion of pluralism. For him, the issue is one of a "pluralistic Christian society" vs. a "secularist unitary society."... If we are truly pluralist in our legal system, then by definition we cannot be, under the law, "Christian."... The opposite of secularism is not Christendom, as he appears to think, but pluralism, under which all religions are equal before the law. In that fact lies the heart of our system.

Ultimately, as Fr. John Courtney Murray, one of the chief architects of the *Declaration on Religious Liberty,* argued, the fundamental dignity of each person is at the heart of all personal freedom. As we reflect on the Holocaust experience we see a special urgency to speak out strongly whenever the basic dignity of any group, especially a group included in the Nazi genocidal plan, is being assaulted. Here I must raise in conscience the issue of the very disturbing violence we have seen directed against the gay community in New York by some Catholics and Jews during the debate over the gay rights legislation. No matter what one's personal stand on the actual legislation, and I support it, there is no room for any condoning or association, even by implication, of religious leadership with the kind of vitriolic hatred that surfaced there if we have truly leaned from the Holocaust experience. As the psychologist Gordon Allport has reminded us, the step from verbal violence to actual violence is short an usually inevitable. In all such situations the moving verses of Pastor Martin Niemoller must be our guide:

> First they came for the Jews
> and I did not speak out—
> because I was not a Jew.
>
> Then they came for the socialists
> and I did not speak out—
> because I was not a socialist.
>
> Then they came for the trade unionists
> and I did not speak out—
> because I was not a trade unionist.
>
> Then they came for me—
> and there was no one left
> to speak out for me.

The task confronting us in the days ahead, my brothers and sisters, may seem overwhelming. Discouragement can easily arise as we look at regressive forces rising in our society at large and even in our respective religious traditions. But even if calculated analysis would seem to dictate pessimism, we need to adopt the perspective of the Italian political theorist Antonio Gramsci who wrote during World War II that this has become a season for "pessimism of the mind, the optimism of the will." May the experience of this workshop renew our hope and give us as Christians and Jews a new collective will for reconciliation.

JEWS, CHRISTIANS AND
A THEOLOGY FOR
THE FUTURE

When Christians Meet Jews

Dr. Paul M. van Buren

We have a remarkable opportunity, in these chapters, to learn something of two millennia of the histories of, and the relationship between, the Church and the Jewish people. I call this opportunity remarkable, because it was one that was not available to me when I was going through my college, seminary and graduate school years. In a sense, we have come a long way, most of it in the last twenty years. But I am not sure we have come all that far that we can turn from the past and look ahead. We are asked to look toward tomorrow. We have so much still to learn, to digest, and to put into action today. So I prefer to stick to a more limited topic: "When Christians Meet Jews." Actual Christians meeting actual Jews: that is real. That actually can and does happen from time to time. In this country, thank God, it happens quite often. I'd like you to reflect for a bit on this fact of our everyday experience, and because it's a strange fact and potentially a deeply disturbing one, I want to share with you some of my thoughts on it.

When Christians meet Jews, the first thing they meet is the reality of another way. In the enthusiasm of what he and his community had been given so recently, the author of the Fourth Gospel presented Jesus as having said, "I am the way.... No one comes to the Father but by me." The remarkable Jewish theologian, Franz Rosenzweig, thought that that verse was true: for Gentiles far from the God of Israel, Jesus has been given as their way to the Father. But of course, he added, the verse does not apply to the Jewish people, for they have always been with the Father from the beginning. Almost fifty years after Rosenzweig wrote that, the Church began slowly to come around to his reading of that verse, but only after nineteen centuries of having read it rather differently.

I think it is worth pointing out that this colossal one hundred and eighty degree turn in Christian teaching concerning the Jews did not come as the idea of some wild-eyed academics or theologians. It came from the Pope and the Bishops of the Second Vatican Council in the Declaration *Nostra Aetate,* October 28, 1965. They didn't spell out what they started, but they were the ones who put us into the turn, and they are the ones who have kept the wheel turning. The Church is still struggling to keep its tires on the track as it tries to complete the maneuver. What the Second Vatican Council has led the Church to see is that when Christians meet Jews, they meet the reality of a living and lived covenant, a way of being human in the service of God, and a way of God's will being done in human life, which was there before there was a Church and will, we must assume, be there as long as history lasts. When Christians meet Jews, they meet the most concrete evidence available to them of the faithfulness of God.

We should not pass too quickly over the concreteness of the persons we meet when we meet Jews. They come in a great variety of sizes and shapes. Anyone who thinks he or she knows what a Jew looks like needs to take a short walk down any of the main streets of Jerusalem and see Jews gathered from a hundred different lands and with as many variations. If one does meet actual Jews, one soon learns that there is no agreement whatsoever among Jews as to what it is to be a Jew. Some are as religious, in our Christian sense of the word, as can be imagined, and others as secular as it is possible to be. Yet they know themselves as Jews. Being Jewish is really not like being Christian. Theirs is truly another way, a different way.

I am talking, of course, about what happens when Christians meet actual Jews. What they do *not* meet are their roots. If Christians want to find their roots, I recommend going to the history books or to a cemetery. Actual Jews are not our roots, my fellow Christians, and we should stop insulting actual Jews by treating them as old roots. That is almost as bad as treating them as types or symbols. Equally, don't think to find out about actual Jews by looking in the Bible. Surely that should have become clear for us through the dialogues of these past few years. The Bible can tell us much about the roots of both Christians and Jews, but actual Jews, like actual Christians, are today the products of over two thousand years of numerous developments since the last word of the Bible was written.

Since actual Jews are the visible aspect of God's gracious covenant, one might conclude that we Christians would be joyful at meeting Jews, yet it is terribly threatening for many of us. For we have thought for so long that ours was the only way, the one true way. And indeed it is—for us. But before God loved us and called us to service through Christ, he had called Israel to be his own and bound himself to the Jewish people with an eternal love. Need the one exclude the other? Only when we make God into our own image and define

God's love as we do our own, on the principle of scarcity. But the God of Israel is evidently a larger God than that, and God's love seems to be able to cover more than ours.

So God is larger and more inclusive than we thought? If so, it follows that the Church is surely smaller than we had thought. One of the inevitable implications of the Church's belated acknowledgement of the eternity of the covenant between the God we worship, the God of Israel, and the Jewish people, is that we need to have a more realistic ecclesiology or doctrine concerning who we are as Christians. If the Jewish people are and remain the people of God, then who are we? Clearly we are not Jews, for we were called, if the calling of the apostle Paul was authentic, to serve God as Gentiles. There may be Jews among us, as there are baptized persons who have become Jews. After long reflection on these exceptions, however, and after talking with a number of them, I have come to the conclusion that we are seriously mistaken if we call them converts, which is the popular term for them. How can you convert from serving the God of Israel in one way to serving the God of Israel in another? No, I think it wiser to say that some individuals have special callings from God concerning how they are to serve him, and the Pharisee Paul and the Galilean fisherman called Rocky (Peter, that is) were only the first of many examples.

As a rule, however, we need to realize that we Christians are Gentiles called to serve the God of Israel alongside of and in no sense in the stead of the Jewish people of God. Our blessing is that, not being descendants of Abraham, we have as Gentiles been drafted into the service of Abraham's God and so into a cooperative relationship with the Jewish people. What a scandal that it has taken us nineteen centuries to realize this! We have a lot of catching up to do, and a lot of forgiveness to ask for and amends to make, for what our ancestors in the faith have done to the people of God.

JEWISH DIVERSITY AND UNITY

What do we meet when we Christians meet Jews? We meet, second, something for which we have no single appropriate term. We meet a people, but a people who is in a sense also a nation. We meet a collectivity, or, rather, we meet people who understand themselves to be a collectivity and so can only be fairly understood by us as a collectivity.

One consequence of this is the Jewish concern to have children, to see to it that there will be the next generation. I suppose the response to the Holocaust which has been the most incredibly courageous is at the same time the most fundamentally Jewish: that has been the decision to have children in the face of the annihilation of a third of their people. The will to survive, in its Jewish form, is not personal so much as it is a will that the people Israel survive.

Jews have a deep sense of their corporate identity. They identify with all other Jews, wherever they may be. There is an interesting Jewish question that reveals this: whenever something happens or is proposed to happen, they often ask, "Is it good for the Jews?" Not is it good for me, or my local community, but is it good for the whole people!

"Tribalism!" I hear some Christians say. Well, if no more accurate term can be thought of then call it that, but one should know whereof one speaks, and know how different is the Jewish people from the Christian Church. I have met many Jews who were simply appalled to see that Christians in America, for example, showed almost no concern for what has happened to the Christians of Lebanon in recent years. Compare that with the worldwide Jewish concern for the Jews of the Soviet Union. And compare our Christian behavior with the Israeli airlift to rescue the black Jews of Ethiopia. When Christians meet Jews, they meet a "tribe," all right, but a tribe that can expose how superficial is our Christian so-called ecumenicity. And let us not forget whose idea it was that this tribe get started, expand and endure. It wasn't Abraham's idea. No, when Christians meet Jews, they meet a people bound to the only God we know, and so we are constantly reminded that our God is an eternally compromised God, compromised by his promise to be forever the God of this people.

It is important, however, not to idealize Jewish solidarity. When Christians meet Jews, real Jews, they meet a bewildering variety of ways in which to be Jewish. The Jewish people is deeply divided between Orthodox and Reform, between secular and religious, and those on both sides of such lines expend an enormous amount of energy urging their fellow Jews on the other side to be Jewish in *their* way. Yet when there is a threat to any Jews, the sense of unity seems to take over. The Jews, in all their differences, are one in a way that is rare among Christians.

I have touched on this matter of Jewish solidarity because it is so evident in Jewish attitudes toward the Jewish state which Christians almost invariably run into when they meet Jews. I want to turn to Zionism and the State of Israel, then, as that which many Christians seem to find the most difficult aspect of their meeting with Jews. It is today and will continue to be tomorrow such a central matter when Christians meet Jews.

THE STATE OF ISRAEL

When Christians meet Jews, they are soon confronted with Jewish loyalty to and concern for the State of Israel. In short, they run into, or they go to inordinate lengths to pretend they have not run into, Zionism. I think we had better look more closely at this.

Medinat Yisrael (The State of Israel) is in large part the consequence of the Zionist movement, which came into being to encourage a Jewish return to and possession of *Eretz Yisrael* (The Land of Israel). In its goal to have all Jews return, and in its hope thereby to put an end to antisemitism, Zionism has been a failure, but in its central goal to re-establish the Jewish people in their own, ancient land, it has succeeded. Although Zionism is a modern movement, its roots are as old as the Jewish people themselves. Indeed, the promise of this particular land to this particular people is a central feature of the tradition's story of its very beginning: it is there in the first words spoken by God to Abram, even before he is renamed Abraham. Since the Roman expulsion of the Jews from this land by Hadrian, the longing to return has remained central in Jewish piety and prayer. Zionism is therefore rooted in the central traditions of the Jewish people, and, in a general sense, all Jews are Zionists. Insofar as the Church acknowledges the Jews as the people of God's eternal covenant—and that is exactly what the Church has acknowledged, beginning with *Nostra Aetate*—it has no choice but to respect the attachment of this people to that land, because that land is there in the center of that covenant.

Essential to the covenant is the fact of an actual, physical nation/people, the Jews, and an actual piece of real estate, from Dan to Beersheba; its borders may be ever in flux, but its specificity is never in doubt. To a remarkable extent, the Torah is a constitution for living in and taking care of that land. For the Jewish tradition, therefore, Torah, people and land belong inseparably together. The impact of modernity on the Jewish people may have left them divided over how to live their fidelity to Torah, both in Israel and in the Diaspora, but they are united in fidelity to their people and so to the Jewish State. Torah fidelity, in various forms and with various understandings, still marks the Jewish way of life for many, but Jewish solidarity marks the lives of just about all Jews. The murder of a third of all the Jews in the world in the Holocaust has only heightened the importance which almost all Jews attach to the survival of the State of Israel and accounts for their political agenda, which has as its highest priority the defense of this priceless reality.

For Jews to be in their land under present world conditions is hard to imagine unless they could be there under their own control. It means, in short, a Jewish State. The consequence, inevitably, is ambiguity, an ambiguity made explicit by the name which its secular Jewish founders chose for it: Israel. However difficult it may be for the traditional Christian reading of the Hebrew Bible, Israel is again back on the plane of history, as it so clearly was in the time of Israel's Scriptures. Can this Israel be that Israel? Can the ways of God with this world really have anything to do with statesmanship, treaties, political parties and economic policy? The Jewish State, where

Jewish guards oversee Jewish prisoners in Jewish jails for breaking Jewish laws, where an actual Jerusalem has to be run like any city, with all the problems of any urban center, poses a fundamental question about the place of ambiguity in our understanding of God and God's dealings with this world.

Before discussing this question, however, it should be acknowledged that many Christians do not see any particular importance, and, therefore, nothing of theological significance, in the State of Israel, because they take it to be a merely political entity, a state like any other state. This position is logically connected with a reading of Israel's Scriptures as the "Old Testament," so we must pause to consider this problem before proceeding.

The Scriptures which Jews and Christians share are of course Israel's first of all, for they were written by Jews, preserved by Jews and addressed to Jews. They were all written before there ever was a church. They are the storehouse of Israel's memories of its own past history with God and of God's history with this his people. They are Israel's earliest memories of and reflection upon the oldest, longest and stormiest love affair of recorded history, that between God, the Creator of the heavens and the earth, and Israel the people of his choice, a love affair still going on to this day, with all its ups and downs, between the Jewish people and their God, the God of Israel.

Because Jesus and all his disciples were Jews, he and they too read the Scriptures as their own. Consequently, the Gentile members of Christ's body, the church, by their promised adoption as younger sisters and brothers of Jesus, also read them as their own. And yet, that is not quite right. That passes too easily over the fact that, in a definite sense, these writings remain Israel's and can therefore only be read by the Church as Israel's. When the Church reads these writings, it is overhearing a conversation, sometimes a lovers' quarrel, but always a dialogue between partners of which it must acknowledge that it is not one. The partners in this conversation, be it joyful or fearful, are God and Israel.

We find ourselves here near the center of that miracle which is the faith and life of the Gentile Church: the Church believes itself to be invited and authorized to *overhear* Israel's conversation with God, and God's conversation with Israel, as a matter in which it is included. The Church believes itself to be an authorized eavesdropper on this love affair, authorized to hold the incredible conviction that it too is addressed by God's words of love addressed to Israel, that it too is reproved by God's words of stern reproof to Israel, that it too has a part to play, alongside of Israel, in the story which began to unfold with the call of Abraham.

The grounds for this incredible conviction can be no other than the Church's foundational conviction that Jesus was and is the Anointed of God, authorized to speak and act in the name of the One God and to confront them with the gift and claim of God's unbounded love. In acknowledging Jesus to be that, the Church discovers itself as also a hearer of the Word of God and so an *over*hearer of the story which Israel's Scriptures tell of God's love affair with Israel.

For the Church, the miracle of miracles is not that there should have been apostles, witnesses to God's affirmation of the Crucified as his Anointed One, but that there should have been an apostle to the *Gentiles*. In the apostolic story of Jesus, as in Israel's Scriptures, the bread is truly for the children, for Israel; the miracle is that there are crumbs for Gentile dogs, indeed that the dogs are no longer called dogs, but friends, brothers and sisters of Jesus, and so, although Johnny-come-latelies, nevertheless invited to hold tightly to the hem of the garment of this Jewish older brother, and to learn to understand themselves as sharing with him in Israel's story and the love affair between God and the Jewish people which he is authorized to embody for them.

The Church was therefore being faithful to its foundation in claiming Israel's Scriptures as its own. It did not think to make clear, however—as Paul's worries on the subject in his letter to the Romans do make clear—that it claimed them as *also* its own. It learned from them to speak of God, but it forgot that the vocabulary with which it learned to do so was a Jewish one. It failed to recall that the promises of God were first of all explicitly for the Jewish people, and it did not see that if these promises were ever to lose their specificity (remember that piece of real estate?), then the story, which they have felt authorized to consider as also their own, would lose its concrete grounding in this world and so would cease to be a real story, a story of reality.

So it came about that the Scriptures of Israel, and so of Jesus and his disciples, became the "Old Testament" of the Gentile Church. In its early struggles with Gnosticism, the Church mishandled badly the issue raised by Marcion and his followers at the beginning of the second century of our Common Era. Marcion at least read the Scriptures as they had been intended originally. He seems to have been the only Christian leader of his day, as Professor Pelikan has pointed out, to have recognized that the Scriptures were Israel's, unquestionably the Bible of the Jews. On that starting point at least, he was historically and theologically correct. His mistake was to conclude that the Church should have nothing to do with those Jewish writings. He had obviously missed completely the point of the apostle to the Gentiles, that this root really was the support of the Church, that the Gentiles had been grafted into the root or trunk of God's dealings with Israel of which the Jewish Scriptures tell. The "Orthodox" leaders, however, in rejecting Marcion's conclusion, rejected also his sound starting point. They denied that the Scriptures were primarily Israel's, promising, for example, an actual piece of real estate to an actual nation/people, and turned them instead into the Church's Old Testament, with its promises spiritualized and allegorized so as to make them directly and originally promises to the Gentile Church. Thus in winning the battle with Marcion, the Church lost the war with Gnosticism. Christian anti-Zionism of today is but a part of our present payment on the colossal debt to Gnosticism incurred in the second century.

The State of Israel, to return to my main subject, raises the important theological question of ambiguity, precisely as a modern, "secular" state established by Jewish blood, sweat and tears, and maintained against the wishes of hostile neighbors by the Israel Defense Force, in precisely the Land of Promise, which is also the area which Gentiles have called Palestine and which Palestinian Arabs claim as their land. As any visitor can hardly fail to note, everything about Israel is ambiguous. What the Christian can learn from this, however, is that Israel's whole story from the beginning has been ambiguous, as ambiguous as the Church's story of Jesus of Nazareth and his death and resurrection. The great difference between those ancient stories and the story unfolding in our days is that today we hear so much more of the present tale that we have difficulty hearing it as a story at all, especially as a fresh new chapter of the old story.

For example, in the biblical account, we hear only Israel's story of the conquest of the Land under Joshua, without a word from a Canaanite Liberation Organization. We can laugh and love with the colorful, almost bawdy story of Samson, but a Philistine Liberation leader would have had another tale to tell. In the Bible, we hear only of David's taking of Jerusalem; today we can hear the Jebusite version, as well, and see it all on television, with endless, acrimonious debates aired in the United *Goyim* ("Nations") Organization. We get a fuller picture today, we may think. Are we not still posed with the question of what is really going on?

Much recent theology is plagued with a suspicion that the problem with God's mighty works of old are that they are just that: old. God does not intervene in history the way he used to, we seem to think. Yet I suggest that precisely the modern Jewish State challenges this skepticism. It can remind us that it took a certain eye to see David as God's anointed, rather than as a Benjaminite terrorist. As for Moses on Mount Sinai, there was so little to see there of God's mighty act that most of those present gave up on Moses completely, being, rather like us, only able to take seriously an unambiguously visible God. The Jewish State invites us to see that the God of Israel never was that sort of God and never acted of old as that sort of God. He is and has always been a more ambiguous operator than that, and if we cannot dare to see his hand in events of our day, we delude ourselves and misread Israel's Scriptures if we think that that hand was ever obvious. For those with eyes to see, there is a mystery about the Jewish State. Its secular founders gave it a name that should alert us to that mystery. Behind that name "Israel" lurks a memory of a Presence that threatens us with the possibility that God may not be as comfortably far from this world as we moderns might wish him to be. What then are we to say to that favorite Christian question, whether we have the right to criticize the actions and policies of Israel? The right to criticize the Jewish people is one that Christians, more than all others, have to earn, if their criticism is to be anything more than one more expression of the Church's long-standing and long discredited anti-Judaism. Criticism by the disciples of a Gentile, anti-Judaic Jesus (based on their reading of their anti-Judaic "Old Testament") will be properly ignored by Israelis, who have more than enough criticism to digest from those (primarily Israeli) critics who have earned the right to raise questions about how to relate responsibly to those who refuse even to recognize Israel's right to exist. Critics who have not earned the right to speak, of whom there have always been more than enough, may satisfy their own needs to gratify their own self-righteousness, but they will contribute nothing positive to the immensely difficult task which has fallen to the Jews of being a people bound by such a covenant to such a partner in such a world.

In the meantime, it behooves any Christian to learn the history of the Jewish people, including especially their history under Christian domination, and to learn the history of the founding of Israel and of the war that its Arab neighbors have been waging against it ever since. What goes on today in Israel is so shaped by that history that to speak in ignorance of it is simply stupid. When one learns that history, one is relieved of the Christian obsession with criticizing Israel. Of course Israel is not perfect. Of course its leaders have made mistakes and will surely make more. Can Christians really believe that the people whose ancestors wrote and preserved the Scriptures, and who revere them still today, need us to point this out to them?

A LIVING COVENANT

When Christians meet Jews, they run into—among other things—another way, a people, and the Zionist State. They are thereby invited to see that God is larger, more compromised, and much more ambiguous in his actions than we have generally held in our theologies. Before closing with a practical suggestion for the future, I want to sum up all that I believe to be involved in our meetings with Jews by pointing out we are really running into what my colleague David Hartman has used as the title for his excellent book: when Christians meet Jews, they run into a living covenant.

Covenant: I shall be your God and you shall be my people. covenant is first of all a gift. Covenant means that there is provided a way to walk, a way to live, a way to be human, a way to be a community. The covenant is God's gracious gift to the Jewish people of genuine responsibility for the present and the future. A path has been provided, the walking of which is for this people the service of God. Covenant means you don't have to stop and nervously take your spiritual temperature every five minutes to see whether you believe what you are supposed to believe. Covenant means that there are things to be done no matter what your immediate spiritual state, and you are free to do them. It means the joy of having the religious question off your back, so that you can put one foot in front of the other and get on with the task of living. Covenant means the gracious free gift of God's commandments, lots of commandments, six hundred and thirteen of them, all sorts of things to do, and every single one of them a way in which to serve God.

But Covenant also means two-sidedness. Covenant means that life is not only a gift but also a responsibility. The covenant is not in the heavens but on earth, here in the actual life of actual Jews. Better than Powder Milk Biscuits, the Torah gives Jews the courage to get up and do the things that need to be done. The covenant means shared responsibility. It means that you don't leave everything to God. God's gracious covenant means that God graciously does not want to have his people live by grace alone. God wants his creatures to get up on their own feet and walk.

Christians are sometimes inclined to worry about why God seems so seldom to do what we ask of God. When Christians meet Jews, they can begin to learn a new way to think about God's grace and God's actions. The covenantal answer appears to be that God wants us to do more of what we ask of God. That certainly does not mean that we should pray less. On the contrary, God wants us to pray so hard that we begin to see what we should do about the situation.

Second, when Christians meet Jews, they run up against a *living* covenant. The covenant is alive, and it is being lived right now, today. The covenant is the Jewish people's constitution, and so, like any constitution that is alive, it is constantly being renewed by adapting it to new situations. Torah, like any constitution, is truly conserved only when it is being renewed by creatively working out new ways to meet new challenges. That is what the whole history of Judaism has been, and that is what the so-called Oral Torah has been about. The Talmud, and the ongoing discussion about how the Torah is to be interpreted, is one long history of a living constitution in action. The divisions within Judaism are so many signs that the political reality of the covenant is alive that the old covenant is ever becoming a new covenant. The liveliness of Jewish debate about Torah is evidence that the covenant is alive, that the story begun with Abraham is still being written, and not least in the new chapter presently being lived and argued about in the Jewish state. What Christians meet when they meet Jews is a living covenant, one that should open our eyes to see that it is really our God-given responsibility to decide what the Word of God is and ought to be in our present situation.

Finally, when Christians meet Jews, they run into a living covenant, just one. On the whole, Jews have not held that their Way is the only way for all humanity. They have held that their Way is the only way for them. They sort of think it's the best way, naturally, but they have resisted universalizing their own particularity. They have had the humility to allow that God may have other ways of relating to other peoples. I think that there lies in this fact one of the great lessons that we Christians need to ponder today and will need to ponder tomorrow.

As I read our Scriptures and tradition, I am convinced that we can only speak properly of one single covenant, that between God and Israel, begun with Abraham, renewed and given much more content at Sinai, but then renewed again and again throughout the long history of God with this people, and this people with God, to our day. From this quite particular covenant, we learn of God's maternal concern for all of creation, so why should we ever think that God has not some particular concerns for the people of China, for example, or for the peoples of the Indian sub-continent? Just because the one covenant gives little or no information on such matters does not entail that God's concern is limited only to Israel.

As for ourselves, the Gentile Church, I believe that we are the fruit of one of the many renewals of the one covenant. It turned out strangely, but then so have many other creative renewals of that covenant. This particular renewal led to a new entity called the Church, consisting of Gentiles mostly, who found in one Jew an opening to the knowledge and love of the God of the covenant, and a calling to serve that God in a Gentile way. It is a tragedy of major proportions that we failed for so long to see that this was the universal God's particular calling for us, alongside Israel's particular calling. If we are beginning to see that now, it is because Christians have begun in the last couple of decades finally to meet Jews and so discover a living covenant.

DIALOGUE FOR THE FUTURE

I want to conclude by offering a suggestion for how we should proceed with the meeting of Jews and Christians after today. I certainly believe we should go on meeting, because we each have so much to learn that we need to learn from the other. But I think that what we generally call the Jewish-Christian dialogue is coming to the point at which we need even more to do some caucusing. I must leave to Jews to decide how it goes among them and what they think they need to discuss among themselves, but I am quite sure that the meetings with Jews that have been going on over the past twenty years or so have raised some of the profoundest issues that have ever confronted the Christian Church, issues that we need to thrash out among ourselves.

Back in 1967, at an early stage of the dialogue, the Faith and Order Commission of the World Council of Churches tried to face up to the question of the relationship between the Churches and the Jewish people and found that they were unable to come to a common mind on the matter. The conclusion of their report explains why, and in words that bear repeating: "The conversation among us," they said, referring to the conversation among Christians concerning their relationship to the Jewish people, "has only just begun, and we realize that in this question the entire self-understanding of the Church is at stake." Truer words were never written. But just because so much is at stake, and just because Christians are not yet of one mind on this question, I am inclined to believe that further progress in the relationship will depend on Christians getting off by themselves and seeing if they can learn to listen to each other.

I don't think Jews realize how threatening they have been for Christians down through the centuries. Since for most of that time the Church held the upper hand, numerically, politically and economically, the Church was able to be and was a terrible threat to Jews. So tangible was that threat, and so real was Christian persecution of Jews, that Jews have not seen that part of the force of that persecution came from the insecurity of Christians in the face of the people who really were Abraham's descendants, who really did know the language of Moses and of the prophets, and who really could and did continue to call themselves Israel. Behind the Christian denial of Jewish legitimacy lurked the fear of their own illegitimacy.

Through the process of dialogue, this fear can in part be faced and put to rest, but because it is not fully dead, I believe that we Christians need to do some caucusing among ourselves as we work at coming to a self-understanding of the Church that not only allows room but positively creates room, as a prime necessity of our own identity, for the presence of the Jewish people. I offer that suggestion for consideration, in the service of the developing friendship between the Church and the Jewish people, of which the Ninth National Workshop has been such a helpful expression.

Judaism Encounters Christianity Anew

Rabbi David Hartman

Had I been living prior to the existence of the State of Israel, I would not begin the very difficult process of an agonizing reappraisal of the Judaic tradition's perception of Christianity. How dare I suggest a new appreciation of Christianity in light of Jewish suffering in history? How dare I do more than dwell on the haunting memories of the past? I would rather preserve total silence. But I live in Jerusalem. My life is defined by the challenge of belonging to a people that has been blessed with political self-determination. Living in that reality, one is challenged to attempt cautiously a new beginning of our attitudes to other faith communities. This new beginning is made possible by the gift of the living people of Israel, who try desperately to make sense of their own destiny and to build a political reality sensitive to the religious sensibilities of other faith communities.

How the traditional *halakhists* (interpreters of the Torah, oral and written) have viewed Christianity can be exemplified by two major Judaic thinkers: Maimonides and my own rebbe, Rabbi Joseph Soloveitchik. In medieval *halakhic* discussions, the question posed about Christianity was: Does belief in the Trinity constitute a violation of the monotheistic principle? In other words, is Christianity to be considered idolatry and in what sense? How do Jews accordingly apply the biblical and talmudic injunction concerning idolatry? In some commentaries within the Askenazic *halakhic* tradition, compromises were found on how one is to allow for social and economic intercourse with Christianity. Maimonides, however, categorically considered Christianity to be idolatry from the *halakhic* perspective.

But when Maimonides is less concerned with the *halakhic* discussion regarding the notion of idolatry, one can find in his writings two other different responses to Christianity. One occurs in his *Epistle to the Jews of Yemen,* where he writes to a Jewish community terrified by oppression and the threat of forced conversion to Islam. He offers a theological perspective on the role of Christianity and Islam in history, claiming that since the covenantal election of Israel at Sinai there have been many attempts to destroy God's vision for history. The most destructive attempt, more so than the arguments of the pagan philosophers or the political oppression of the Babylonians, has been the scheme of first Christianity and then Islam to undermine God's covenantal vision of history by offering the counterclaim that they have superseded Israel as the elect community, that they are the true inheritors of Sinai through a new revelatory dispensation. The demonic spirit behind that scheme is so intense, says Maimonides, that if they cannot defeat Israel, they prefer to be destroyed together with Israel. For they make people ask themselves: How is it possible for God to tell each of several communities that it and it alone will always enjoy this unique favor? The very existence of the counterclaims to possess total revealed truth undermines the positions of all the claimants.

> Thus doubts will be generated and confusion will be created, since one is opposed to the other and both supposedly emanated from one God, and it will lead to the destruction of both religions. This is a remarkable plan contrived by a person who is envious and malicious, who will strive to kill his enemy and remain alive, and if he cannot achieve this, he will devise a scheme whereby they both will be slain.

The other suggestion he makes occurs in the *Mishneh Torah*, his code of Judaic law, in the section on the Laws of Kings. It is found in a Yemenite manuscript that escaped censorship. Here he offers a perception of Christianity and Islam which has been mistakenly compared with Hegel's "cunning of reason."

> But it is beyond the human mind to fathom the designs of the Creator; for our ways are not His ways, neither are our thoughts His thoughts. All these matters relating to Jesus of Nazareth and the Ishmaelite [Muhammad] who came after him, only served to clear the way for King Messiah, to prepare the whole world to worship God with one accord, as it is written: For then will I turn to the peoples a pure language, that they may all call upon the name of the Lord to serve Him with one consent [Zeph. 3:9]. Thus the messianic hope, the Torah, and the commandments have become familiar topics—topics of conversation [among the inhabitants] of the far isles and many peoples, uncircumcised of heart and flesh. They are discussing these matters and the commandments of the Torah. Some say: "Those commandments were true, but have lost their validity and are no longer binding." Others declare that they had an esoteric meaning and

were not intended to be taken literally, that the Messiah has already come and revealed their occult significance. But when the true King Messiah, will appear and succeed, be exalted and lifted up, they will forthwith recant and realize that they have inherited naught but lies from their fathers, that their prophets and forbears led them astray.

Christianity and Islam, although claiming to supersede Judaism, are really God's instruments for universal messianic redemption through Judaism. For they are spreading the knowledge of the Bible to the whole world, albeit together with their false claim that Israel's suffering shows it to be the rejected people of God. But when the Jews return triumphantly to their own land with the Messianic King, and cease being the despised wanderers in exile, then all the Christians and Muslims will realize that their theologians lied to them and that the truth must be in Judaism.

Maimonides does to Christians what Christians I think have done to Jews, when they treated our history as a prologue on the way to the full flowering of God's redemption in Christianity. Medieval theological discussions often show total blindness to the other.

My own rebbe, Soloveitchik, claims in his article "Confrontation" that one can find room for religious tolerance only in the unredeemed present, while continuing unshakably to believe in eschatological monism. He asserts that it is of the essence of a faith community's commitment to God to believe that ultimately history in its final redemptive moment will justify its own exclusive way and demonstrate the error of all others.

> Second, the axiological awareness of each faith community is an exclusive one, for it believes—and this belief is indispensable to the survival of the community—that its system of dogmas, doctrines and values is best fitted for the attainment of the ultimate good. Third, each faith community is unyielding in its eschatological expectations. It perceives the events at the end of time with exultant certainty, and expects man, by surrender of selfish pettiness and by consecration to the great destiny of life, to embrace the faith that this community has been preaching throughout the millennia. Standardization of practices, equalization of dogmatic certitude, and the waiving of eschatological claims spell the end of the vibrant and great faith experience of any religious community.

The approach to religious pluralism that I shall adopt in this discussion does not presuppose the belief in Jewish Messianic triumphalism. I shall argue, further, that acknowledging the existence of other faiths in their own right need not be a violation of our covenantal faith commitment, but rather the very presence of a dignified other can create within the Judaic spiritual life an enhancement of our covenantal consciousness.

My exposition will be divided into three parts. The first will deal with the theological tension between tradition and modernity. The second will discuss the way in which the State of Israel is a catalyst for a new covenantal self-understanding. Finally, I shall offer directions for a new religious sensibility which can live with uncertainty and ambiguity. I believe that unless there is not only a shift in theological doctrine, but also a radical psychological shift in the human religious sensibility, pluralism will be a vague and vacuous phrase not corresponding in any way to lived reality.

1. THEOLOGICAL TENSION:
THE INDIVIDUAL AND THE COMMUNITY

There is an inner tension that fills the spiritual life of one nurtured by a living tradition like Judaism. The tradition provides the very framework for our spiritual self-understanding. It provides the cultural ambience, the language, the theological categories, the way in which we begin the spiritual life. In contrast to Descartes, we do not find self-identity through a retreat to the bare self of *cogito ergo sum*. One who lives within the Judaic tradition begins by being claimed, together with other members of the community, by God. Fundamentally, the point of departure for Jewish religious consciousness is communal and historical. We begin by listening together to God, by being situated in the framework of a community of listeners.

> You stand this day, all of you, before the Lord your God—your tribal heads, your elders and your officials, all the men of Israel, your children, your wives, even the stranger within your camp, from woodchopper to waterdrawer—to enter into the covenant of the Lord your God, which the Lord your God is concluding with you this day, with its sanctions, to the end that He may establish you this day as His people and be your God, as He promised you and as He swore to your fathers, Abraham, Isaac, and Jacob. I make this covenant, with its sanctions, not with you alone, but with those who are standing here with us this day before the Lord our God and with those who are not with us here this day. [Deut. 29:9-14].

Only within that community is it possible to hear the living God. The *mitzvah*—God's commandment—becomes a living reality only because I am connected to a family. Only within that family is it possible for me to affirm a living spiritual reality. The sin of the wicked son in the story in the Passover Haggadah is his separation from community. Whoever excludes himself or herself from total identification with the community has no access to the *halakhic* way to God. Heresy in Judaism is imagining that the self alone is addressed by God.

There is, however, a strange paradox here. On the one hand, the community is so much of one's essence that one's primary consciousness is of a "we." I am a "we" before I become an "I", and that "I" surfaces only in the tension with the "we." The "I" in Judaism is so difficult to discover that Spinoza believed that there was not an "I" at all, that there was no allowance for a moral sense, and that fundamentally Judaism could only be understood in collective political legal categories. The whole modern critique of Judaism has been that *halakhah* so collectivizes the religious consciousness that there is no autonomous moral self in this tradition. In terms of the Kantian contrast between heteronomy and autonomy, it is claimed, there is no autonomous moral personality within the Jewish framework. In a certain sense, this is true for one who lives in Judaism. Buber, who sought immediacy in the revelatory moment, was therefore really outside of the *halakhic* tradition. The Jew does not begin with immediacy, but by listening to a story from his or her parents, by first participating in the drama of the collective standing before God at Sinai. On the other hand, the Midrash says that each Jew standing at Sinai hears the Word of God in terms of his or her own individual sensibility. The word of revelation, it says, is similar to the manna in the desert: just as each person claimed that the manna tasted of something else, in accordance with his or her own fantasy, so each heard God saying "I am the Lord *thy* God" (Ex. 20:1)—not *your* God in the plural—and the Ten Commandments go on to say "Thou shalt... Thou shalt..." The hearing is individualistic even though the content is totally collective.

> The divine word spoke to each and every person according to this particular capacity. And do not wonder at this. For when manna came down for Israel, each and every person tasted it in keeping with his own capacity—infants in keeping with their capacity, young men in keeping with their capacity, and old men in keeping with their capacity.... Now if each and every person was enabled to taste the manna according to his particular capacity, how much more and more was each and every person enabled according to his particular capacity to hear the divine word. Thus David said: "The voice of the Lord is in its strength" (Ps. 29:4)—not "The voice of the Lord in His strength" but "The voice of the Lord in its strength"—that is, in its strength to make itself heard and understood according to the capacity of each and every person who listens to the divine word. [Pesikta de Rav Kahana, *piska* 12].

The Midrash highlights an inner tension which is always there. Can you build an "I" in a context of being totally claimed by three thousand years of history? Nietzsche struggled with this in his important essay on "The Use and

Abuse of History." Can you on one level be rooted totally in a community, and yet on another level find identity as an individual? Or is rebellion essential for a person's sense of self, because as long as that person is in the context of a traditional community, the self is crushed by the weight of the previous experience? Do you need to distance yourself through total rejection in order to begin to surface as a self? This is a central question for the Judaic tradition. Can you be a self, can you be an "I," a person in the presence of God, and yet be greatly claimed by your *halakhic* tradition?

The two aspects appear also when the election and the covenant are recalled in Deuteronomy.

> The Lord did not set His love upon you or choose you because you were more in number than any people: for you were the fewest of all peoples. But because the Lord loved you, and because He would keep the oath that He had sworn to your ancestors... [Deut. 7:7-8].

On the one hand, God had said to Israel: "I chose your ancestors and this is why I am connected to you." It is because of his love for Abraham, Isaac and Jacob that he feels bound to Israel. On the other hand, the text recalls God saying: "not because you were many, not because you were more powerful, but because I loved you." He begins with his love to Israel and then goes on to add "and because of my covenant with your ancestors." There is an immediacy of God's love: he loves us not just because Jews are the children of Abraham, Isaac, and Jacob.

Although the individual level is there, however, the covenant of the ancestors—*brit avot*—has played an essential role in supporting belief in the eternity of the covenant. The covenant is unconditional because of God's promise to Abraham. One is confident that one is accepted by God because of the memory of Araham's covenant. Because I begin with Abraham's covenant, accordingly, in whatever I do as a philosopher, I must bring a hundred generations into my discussion. My grandfather must understand what I am speaking about. I cannot just do my own thing, without making the effort to make it intelligible to him. In other words, a Jew's self-assertion has to be inside the family. This is why much of Jewish philosophy takes the form of midrashic exegesis. The self does not emerge only in rebellion, but in intellectual struggle to unfold and clarify in a new way what your grandfather said. Even if he did not say it, at least he should be able to feel that you are speaking in his language (cf. Menahot 29b).

This theological framework finds expression in the moment of God's encounter with Moses at the burning bush, when he gives Moses two messages for the children of Israel. First, *Ehyeh asher ehyeh* (Ex. 3:14), which I prefer to understand in the Mekhilta and Judah Halevi sense as "I will be present for you in the future." This, he says, is his name: *Ehyeh*—"I will be." But also he says: "I am the God of Abraham, the God of Isaac and the God of Jacob" (Ex. 3:15). These two messages go together. He is the God of history and community, the God of the covenant of the ancestors, but also a God who says that radical novelty and surprise are possible in a spiritual life in which the covenantal ancestors follow you constantly. "I will be—I will come in new ways." There are new possibilities in a living tradition which are not exhausted by the past. Therefore, Jews have to live in a dialectical tension, feeling surprise, wonderment and openness to what new possibilities will arise, and at the same time feeling totally claimed by the vision of Abraham, Isaac and Jacob.

Before proceeding further, I want to make the following digression in order to avoid any misunderstanding. In my approach to the way the rebirth of Israel calls one to a new appreciation of Judaism, I do not offer a Hegelian kind of judgment about how history is unfolding. I am a rabbinic Jew who believes that Torah "is not in heaven" (Deut. 30:12) and that it is not my task to intuit the divine scheme for history. Nor am I free from making judgments about how I must live by the Halakhah in the everyday. Therefore I am speaking as a committed religious Jew who wants to respond to his reality, who lives in the context of a particular moment of history and has to ask himself what is religiously possible for him at that moment. So I am not making a metaphysical judgment as to how God acts in history, but offering a human halakhic response to history.

2. THE STATE OF ISRAEL AND THE SPIRITUAL GHETTO

Nowhere is the tension between tradition and modernity to be felt more strongly than today in the State of Israel and above all in its capital Jerusalem. One senses in Jerusalem that something radically new is being demanded of the Judaic spirit. It is hard to articulate it clearly, but a Jew living there can feel that something explosive is beginning in the new reality of the ingathering of exiles.

On one level, Jews from everywhere have come home. No more does one meet one's people in history through praying for the ingathering of exiles. Yet only in the home to which we have returned do we find that we are actually so divided. Here we may even wonder: Have we really been a family? The United Jewish Appeal's slogan "We are one" sounds questionable when Jew meets Jew and wonders if we can understand each other. The most serious question in Israel is: Could the chronic dissension turn into a civil war? The polarization between religious and secular is great and increasing. In the newspaper, the big issues are not so much political, but whether the cable car will run on the Sabbath in Haifa and whether a Petah Tikvah cinema will show a film this Friday night. The chief rabbi of the town, locked in jail for leading a violent illegal demonstration against the opening of that cinema, claims to be above the law of the state because he is speaking in the name of God. Four hundred policemen could not spend the Sabbath with their children because they were trying to prevent Jews from fighting with one another.

Immense anger arose some time ago about the question of moving the clock to summertime. Then Interior Minister Peretz, who had the legal responsibility for deciding when summertime should start, belonged to an ultra-Orthodox political party whose highest authority is a group of Torah sages. He did not want to move the clock because then the Sabbath would end one hour later and many young people would be liable to violate the Sabbath by going to cinemas before sunset. But secular groups argued that an earlier start to the day would save 10 million dollars worth of electricity used for air conditioning and that the roads would be safer. As Peretz continued to delay, trade unions and manufacturers and the post office and others began to announce unilateral summertime, maybe as much to spite the ultra-Orthodox as to help the economy. Finally, the cabinet went through a great session and voted for summertime against Minister Peretz's will. One is inspired in such a crisis to sing "we shall overcome."

The reader may be thinking that I am telling a fairy tale but I am talking about lived reality. Anger, cynicism and intense levels of polarization arise over these burning issues between brothers and sisters who have come home after praying so long for the ingathering of exiles.

We have realized our dreams of returning to our covenantal biblical land, only to find that there are Arabs who also feel a deep affection for that land. We have come home to be forced immediately to face another who feels rooted to that same land. Jew and Jew meet each other in their otherness; Jew and Arab are suddenly cast together in a common destiny.

In this land, we are confronted with so many others who have different experiences connecting them to it. The Mormons start to build a university in Jerusalem and many Jews try to stop them, claiming it to be a missionary plot. The muezzin calls thousands of Muslims to their mosques as thousands of Hasidim go to the Western Wall. Believers of different faiths rub against each other in the alleys of the Old City; different religious musics ring out simultaneously.

We have come home, yet to a home which does not offer us security and serenity, but forces us to meet the other. The other invades our self-definition. Usually, when people come home, they free themselves from having to integrate all the dissonant sounds that are heard outside. The paradox is that it was easier to do that when we lived in the Diaspora, because there we could build a ghetto. The ghetto is not defined just by a physical area. The ghetto allowed Jews to define themselves in their own language without having to meet otherness. The ghetto provided an opportunity to build a cultural self-definition in which all that surrounded us confirmed our own internal communal language, in which cultural monism was possible, in which all that surrounded us was internal to your family. In Jerusalem, I come home and I am invaded by multiple experiences of radical diversity.

Our return to the land is the greatest testimony of our people's belief in God's dream. My understanding of prophecy is that it was the intuition of Moses to hear God's prayer that Israel shall be a holy people. Moses heard that prayer and we are burdened forever with trying to translate it into the concrete. Election is not a description of ontological uniqueness, as Judah Halevi claimed, but the principle of God's dream and prayer for history. Yet when we come home, hoping for another change to realize that dream and prayer, no one around wants us to be there. What a horrible experience, when no one in our whole Middle Eastern environment speaks as if we were there. Cities like Tel Aviv, where hundreds of thousands of Jews live, simply do not appear on Arab maps.

It could be seen most painfully in a Eurovision Song Contest. A simple idea: each nation sends a pop group to sing a song and then all vote on which song was best. Yet it is an amazing thing to see how Israelis watch Eurovision. I am sitting with my son when the German delegation comes to vote. Israel is doing very badly—hardly any delegation has given votes to its song—and when that happens it is like a public desecration of God in history. Then my son says to me: "Germany will have to give us some points after German guilt." What did Britain do to us once? Perhaps we deserve something from them too. But the oddest experience is to watch Eurovision on Jordanian television, which we can receive in Jerusalem, because, strangely enough, in Jordan's Eurovision we were not there. When Israel sang, there was a blank on the screen—"Intermission." We simply were not in the festival. Can you imagine it? You turn to your own country's television, and you hear your song. You turn to Jordan, and you do not exist. We return home, faithful to a promise, to a dream and a prayer. We return into history—and for everyone around us, we become a non-people. Israel is the greatest testimony to a people's loyalty to a covenantal drama, and yet Israel is the greatest testimony of a people in a situation of conflict with its tradition. What a strange dialectic.

As I look at this situation empirically, I see that the God who in the Exodus drama answers "I will be" is calling us to respond in some new way. Something new is happening when the other, the stranger, the different one impinges on our self-definition. Cultural monism is no longer a psychological option in our situation. Therefore, part of the very return of the Jewish people to Israel is the challenge to rethink messianic triumphalism. The very meaning of our return is to find not a haven against antisemitism, but a new way in which the other, the different one, may enter into our consciousness with love rather than suspicion. Can the committed believer, in whatever her or his faith tradition, build an identity in which the other as stranger, as different, is present in his or her own dignity? Or must the religious self, in order for it to experience any dignity, claim absolute universal truth? For me, at any rate, return to the State of Israel entails surrendering the belief that there is one universal scheme for redemption in history.

3. TOWARD A NEW RELIGIOUS SENSIBILITY

What is the new religious sensibility that I believe is now required? We must move away from the longing to be saved from history through eschatology. This move will be possible when we achieve a proper appreciation of the world and humanity as God's creations. Creation is the affirmation not of the exclusive worth of eternity, but of the value of temporality. Creation is the surfacing of the creature who is other than God.

The gnostics could not understand the world as the expression of a loving God. Human suffering, death, tragedy, evil, pain, loving a child and watching him or her die—this could not be the expression of a loving God. The very experience of the world they thought, defies the notion of God as love, and therefore God as love has in some way to be anchored in the drama of eternity. One must get away from the world to discover God as good.

Judaism, however, has affirmed that the creature is good in the eyes of God, as it is said repeatedly in the first chapter of Genesis. God affirms our humanity in its otherness, in its difference, in its finitude. We who are fragile corporeal creatures, who are here today and gone tomorrow, who experience pain, tragedy, loss—this reality is not sin, for "God saw all that he had made, and behold it was very good" (Gen. 1:31). Creation, therefore, is the introduction of a new value in the mind of divinity: temporality, finitude. The human being as a creature is declared to have ontological worth. As the midrash says: "God saw that all he had made was very good." He has seen death and proclaims that also death is good. Accordingly, we do not have to transcend our human finitude in order to feel dignified; we do not have to transcend the concrete and the temporal in order to feel that we are living an authentic life.

The confirmation of human beings in their human limitations is the soul of the covenantal message. The covenant is not God's desire for humanity to escape from history, but God's gracious love saying that humanity in its finite temporal condition is fully accepted by the eternal God. In the covenant, God seeks to enter the temporal; he does not ask the temporal to become absorbed in his eternity. It is in that sense that the covenant—and Buber sensed this— is contrary to the mystical, to the absorption into the One, to the quest to lose individual consciousness. But whereas Buber loved the speech in Exodus 19 which says "I carry you on eagle's wings," I love the story of the manna. God gives manna and asks Israel: "Please, just take enough for one day and trust that tomorrow I will bring you more. But on Friday, take double the amount, and trust that it will last over the Sabbath. So do not go out on the Sabbath to gather manna." It would have been a nice story, had Israel gathered just enough for one day and said: "God, we trust you." But if we look at the story, it goes on: "And Israel nonetheless gathered more than enough manna and tried to set some aside, but it rotted.... Then the Sabbath came and nonetheless they went out." God asks them, so to speak: "Can't you spend one night sleeping with the uncertainty principle and wake up in the morning with radical surprise and wonderment in the sense of Heschel's *God in Search of Man*? Can't you feel this great sense of reverence and wonderment for life?" And their response is: "No. Not that we don't trust you, but...." The amazing thing about the manna story is that it was to these people who could not sleep with uncertainty that God gave the covenant.

The manna story differs significantly from the flood story. In the latter, God creates human beings in the divine image, and has a great dream for what they will be. When they do not turn out the way God thought, divine love turns into divine rage and destroys the world, because great love can turn into hate if it is not grounded in an appreciation of the limitations of the beloved. If you love your dream too much, you destroy reality on its account. Great revolutionaries, in the name of their love for humanity, turn into haters of humanity, because what they love is an abstract dream of humanity rather than an appreciation of what humanity is in the concrete.

The covenant was made in the desert to tell us that God gave up fantasies about what Israel is. Israel in its limitations is accepted by God, as is Israel who builds a golden calf, Israel who wants to go back to Egypt every time water or food is in short supply. Israel in rebellion is still loved, because God's covenant is based on what human beings are like and not on God's expectations for Israel. If it had been God's fantasy, I would be frightened to accept the covenant of Sinai today. But because of the description of Israel's failures, I know God's love is based upon reality. Weak and fragile human beings are given the commandments. So when I put on my *tefillin* in the morning, it is not human grandeur which is confirmed, but human vulnerability, my weakness in which I can nonetheless love God and sense God's acceptance. I am a "commanded one" within the context of human limitations.

The covenant, therefore, signifies for me the re-establishment of the dignity of the concrete. It is the celebration of human finitude. It is the ability to love in spite of human limitations, to build meaning in the face of death, to affirm today without the certainty of tomorrow. George Steiner is mistaken when he claims that "tragedy is alien to the Judaic sense of the world." One just has to read the book of Job to understand that there was never a resolution to Job's problem. At the end of the story, God does not answer Job's questions, but as Maimonides understood, Job gains a new perception of history and of God and goes on (*Guide* 3:23). People may think it is a happy ending, but one who has experienced the death of a child knows how painful it is to love, seeing how death has become a permanent reality. Yet Job had the courage to have a family again, in spite of that uncertainty.

God does not offer us a picture of a worked out framework of meaning. It is not the longing to see certainty, to see a world filled with bliss and beauty, that receives any satisfaction, but only the longing to say there is meaning amidst political corruption, meaning in the crumb. The rabbis in the Talmud rightly understood it when they related how the angels asked God: "Why do you show favoritism to Israel?" God answers: "Shall I not show favoritism to Israel? For I wrote in the Torah: 'And you shall eat and be satisfied and bless the Lord your God' [Deut. 8:10]. But they are able to say grace after eating merely an olive or an egg." I understand this to mean: in the Bible, God promised them a full meal, and only after a full meal did he require them to say grace, but Israel has learned in history to say grace even though they remain hungry.

Can the spiritual life be based upon the fact that I do not have the full meal? I claim that it can, although I understand people who cannot bear the fact that human suffering is not ultimately intelligible as part of some larger scheme. When I was a synagogue rabbi, I could never say to congregants who had some tragedy: "Oh, God just called your child back." I would only weep with my congregants, but I could never offer them the type of comfort that suggests "your child was so loved by God that he wanted it back in heaven." Nor could I find any such comfort as I dedicated my book *A Living Covenant* to the memory of my son-in-law who was killed in war. His death permanently marred my dream for the future.

The existentialists understood something deeply when they said we must live with the understanding of death, but they made the great mistake of making it into the exclusive category of authenticity. Death invades our efforts. It makes all our efforts often appear to be some sort of metaphysical joke. Yet, knowing that we are ants, can we still love? Can we know all our weaknesses and yet take our lives very seriously? Can we live with that tension? I acknowledge that for many people it is impossible. Therefore, they have to believe that in some way there will be a total resolution of the world's madness. There is eternity; there is redemption; there is the ultimate liberation from death. I cannot tell people not to have that sensibility, nor can I disrespect people who have it. But I claim that that sensibility, that longing for eternity and redemption, also created the person who longs for exclusive certainty. The longing to be eternally redeemed can become so profound that you doubt whether your way will take you there if you see another person enjoying his or her different way. The result is then that people have to be deaf to each other's music in order to feel sure that they are saved.

Accordingly, I conclude by asking: Can we love God in an imperfect way and in an imperfect world? Can we experience joy in the spiritual life that we have, yet knowing that it is only a fragment, only a crumb, that God's infinite richness cannot be exhausted by any community in history, that history is not to be understood *sub specie aeternitatis*? History is not the revelation of eternal truth, but God's ability to love us in our imperfection. "The Torah speaks in the language of human beings," as the Torah repeatedly says (cf. *Guide* 3:32). Can we celebrate our finitude, knowing that we remain permanently human, that we never transcend the human in our spiritual life, and that God in his love for us does not ask us to become divine, but to accept ourselves in our own limitation?

Can I love my land, knowing full well that Arabs also must find their dignity in that land? Can they hear my music, allow me to exist in Eurovision? Can they know that I have returned home, yet not in order to say that there is only one redemptive scheme in history, but to offer the world a dignified joyful people who can celebrate and say grace while we are still hungry?

Can I affirm the covenant, knowing that my people have gone through a great spiritual revolution and that there will never be one form of value consensus among the Jewish people? Can I say you are my brother or sister although we do not share the same ritual and the same prayers?

Can I happily see Christians in their passionate love for what mediates the spiritual life for them, can I celebrate their joy and yet not feel that my joy of *mitzvah* is weakened? Can I hear the Rev. Coos Schoneveld and Paul van Buren, my teachers in spiritual pluralism, talk about their love for Jesus, can I see their spirituality and integrity, yet without it calling into question my own vitality? Can I continue to appreciate the profound message of my philosophy teacher Robert C. Pollock, of blessed memory, who taught me to listen and appreciate the variety of spiritual rhythms found in the American experience? Do I need the assurance of exclusive truth in order to love God? Can I celebrate Judaism in Jewish life while listening to the other?

I believe that the fear of death is in some important sense similar to the fear many people have of religious pluralism. The consciousness of death awakens fear, uncertainty, loss of control. Similar reactions can arise in a pluralistic society when you meet the other who cannot be absorbed by your own categories. Meeting radical difference shakes your sense of certainty. Can you live with the principle of uncertainty, or must you long for absolute truth which you know is ironclad, in which God says: "Here is my way; if you follow it, you are saved: deviate for a moment, and you are lost"—do I need that to build the spiritual life? Must I believe that ultimately the other is merely an instrument for my own redemption, and that ultimately the end of history will show who was right?

That there may be an alternative religious sensibility, I find in a famous passage in the Babylonian Talmud (Eruvin 13b). The rival schools of Hillel and Shammai were so much in disagreement that the Torah threatened to become two Torahs, with the community divided totally. This dispute ended only when a heavenly voice was heard, saying "These and these are the words of the living God, but the *Halakhah* is according to Hillel." Either would be acceptable, so why did God prefer Hillel? The Talmud answers: because when he used to speak in the house of learning, he would always begin by mentioning Shammai's position first. He was so "kindly and modest" that when he spoke to his students, he told them first the contrary view and argued for its plausibility, and only then he presented his own opinion. He never taught Torah pretending to possess the unique truth, but admitting that two opinions might have plausibility and meaning. So let us also belong to teachers who taught a way of commitment to Judaism and the love of God, while maintaining the unsettling assertion that "these and these are the words of the living God."

Appendix: Strategies for the Jewish-Christian Encounter: The Baltimore Experiment

Christopher Leighton

The task of configuring a National Workshop brings out strategists who can plot a course of action with the precision of a military campaign. There is talk of rolling in the big guns, bombarding the audience with challenging ideas, making a obligatory retreat after four days of engagement, and then regrouping in another city in another eighteen months. The organizers of the Ninth National Workshop devoted considerable time and effort contemplating the impact (aftermath) of this academic seige. A small, but diverse nucleus of Christians and Jews from Baltimore turned their attention to the difficult job of regrouping the battered ranks sifting through the fragments left at the conclusion of the conference, and building a new educational enterprise on the territory cleared by the workshop.

Though the image of the battlefield initially appears to contradict the character of interfaith dialogue, many Christians and Jews from the Baltimore community experienced the lectures that are included in this volume and *Interwoven Destinies* as an assault on the way that they have traditionally done business. The discovery that our traditions have sanctioned contempt for the other and that the inheritance lives on in us delivers a jolt to the system. The convulsion shakes the foundations of the faith. A world which once appeared certain and dependable is rocked by doubt and distrust. A dreadful sense of loss is almost inevitable. Some people respond to this disruption by withdrawing into familiar patterns and tightening their defensive positions. Others yield to despair and abandon the tradition. The challenge is to navigate a path through the uncertainty, to hold onto the questions as the old answers flag, and finally to risk and adventure into uncharted theological terrain.

The Institute for Christian and Jewish Studies was established to move the inquiry of the Ninth National Workshop into the depths of the metropolis. From the outset, the ICJS was shaped by an intuition: without sustained local commitment, there would be little possibility of effecting significant change. This experiment would determine whether Christians and Jews could forge a new relationship which would invigorate our religious communities and enrich the quality of interchange among people who see the world differently. The founders of the ICJS recognized at the outset that this theological venture would run aground without the active participation of business leaders as well as educators and clergy from the Jewish and Christian communities.

The linkage between an organization which centers on theological study and the corporate world is not easily fashioned. Resistance often stems from the conviction that religion is a private matter best kept behind closed doors. A pervasive suspicion of religious conversations which spill into the public domain is compounded by a skeptical view of theology. This discipline impresses many people as a relic of medieval scholasticism, an occult science that is dreadfully complex and hopelessly removed from life on the streets.

Yet another obstacle emerges when prospective participants realize that the problem of antisemitism is central to the work of the ICJS. Though this affliction is acknowledged as a serious historical problem, a great many Christians believe that the difficulties are exaggerated. In most professional sectors the walls of discrimination have crumbled. The keys to success are said to belong to Jew and Christian alike. The steady growth in intermarriages seems to demonstrate that anti-Jewish bigotry is a disorder which can only flourish on the fringes of the society. Consequently, an enterprise that focuses on Christian-Jewish relations appears antiquated and parochial. Why not create an organization that places this specific problem of religious pluralism in a broader context? Why not deal with Buddhism and Hinduism, or at least Islam?

Many believe that the democratic experiment in America has inaugurated an era of tolerance. They describe ancient patterns of prejudice as anachronistic. Religious hatred in the New World is gradually yielding to the promise of a society that has learned to keep religion in its place. Why dig on sacred soil when the ground that most Americans till for a living is thoroughly secular? With little time, energy and money available, many people wonder why they should study a disturbing past while the plight of urban America now demands immediate and practical responses.

The Institute for Christian and Jewish Studies could not provide a credible response to these reservations without a coterie of distinguished professional leaders. They have learned to articulate a vision of the ICJS because they have personally experienced the relevance and the urgency of the work. This dynamic of the organization cannot be exaggerated. The momentum which has carried this educational venture into the heart of the community has not come first and foremost from clergy or professional educators, but from well-respected lay leaders who have become convinced that the future of the country in large part turns upon our ability to deal creatively with our religious and ethnic diversity.

The Ninth National Workshop and subsequent involvement with the Institute for Christian and Jewish Studies has presented these community leaders with an opportunity to get to know one another on a level once deemed unattainable. Active participants have come to recognize that you cannot understand a person unless you know the tradition in which the individual stands. You cannot appreciate the values which define a people's character without an appreciation of the history and the ethos of the community to which they belong. In the give and take of the interfaith encounter, the horizons of concern are enlarged. People are impelled to reconsider the boundaries of their identities, to clarify what they believe and why, and to discover the distinctiveness of their own faiths. Such exploration makes possible a level of respect and friendship which many have come to cherish.

Yet a great deal more than self-realization is at stake in this interfaith endeavor. After serving on commissions intended to resolve a failing education system, an epidemic of teenage pregnancies, the proliferation of drugs and the ever increasing outburst of violent crime, a number of ICJS participants have become convinced that no single program or individual will generate a cure for the problems of our cities. Nor will the solutions emerge out of any one philosophy or religion that manages to win or even dictate universal acceptance. Progress will occur to the extent that we learn to tap the wisdom of our various traditions and to forge common commitments in the midst of disagreement. One of the most significant obstacles to this achievement is rooted in the fact that most of us have never learned to engage our own traditions critically, nor have we learned how to argue with our neighbors about our ultimate concerns without losing our civility in the process. The predicament was summarized by Rabbi Michael Cook in his plenary address: "Foremost on our agenda over the next twenty years should be the translation... of scholarship into the *lay* arena." ("A Jewish Approach to Early Christian Writings," *Interwoven Destinies,* Paulist Press/Stimulus, 1993, p. 39.)

The ICJS has developed an educational approach which strives to meet this challenge. Through its various programs, participants are beginning to come to terms with one of the oldest and most intractable pathologies in the western world, the enmity between Christians and Jews. Increasingly, members of the ICJS have come to believe that the religious and ethnic rivalries which splinter communities into warring factions cannot be understood or overcome without a rigorous investigation of Jewish-Christian relations. To walk away from this challenge leads to the abandonment of an invaluable resource, for our religious communities shape our noblest dreams and redefine the borders of our social responsibilities. To ensure the vision of these religious traditions, Christians and Jews will need to discover how to avoid the deadly patterns into which they easily slip when political and economic anxieties intensify.

The fact is difficult to avoid: religious and ethnic antagonisms have generated the vast majority of wars currently raging around the world. Unless religious communities overcome the legacy of bigotry and fanaticism, unless our leaders acknowledge the lethal impact of ignorance and intolerance, our religious communities will continue to ignite embittered struggles at home and abroad. By concentrating on the dynamics of the relationship between Christians and Jews, the ICJS hopes to develop a model of interfaith understanding that will prove adaptable to other communities. This is the dream that has attracted a significant number of professional leaders from Baltimore and prompted them to join clergy and educators in extensive study.

In pursuit of its educational objectives, the ICJS shaped a program which was unique in its scope and design. Though this initiative is known as the Maryland Interfaith Project, the course of study did not follow the normal pattern of an interfaith dialogue. At the outset, twelve individual study groups were divided according to religious affiliation. The ten Christian groups (Roman Catholic, Presbyterian, Lutheran, Methodist, Episcopalian, Southern Baptist, Disciples of Christ, Greek Orthodox, United Church of Christ, and a coalition of African-Americans associated with Coppin State College) were primarily determined by denominational allegiances. The two Jewish groups, one clergy and one lay, included Reform, Conservative, Reconstructionist and Orthodox representatives.

The logic of this configuration stems from an intuition shared by many veterans of the interfaith dialogue. When interfaith gatherings occur, there is an almost irresistible impulse to highlight what everyone has in common. Participants share experiences which lead them to believe that the memories, the beliefs and the practices which divide them into separate camps are really secondary. Deep down everyone is more or less the same. Rather than yield to the climate of gentility, we wanted to create an educational setting in which people could press one another to identify how their religious allegiances distinguish them. We wanted to push participants to discern how the issue of Jewish-Christian relations emerges within their particular tradition.

In the privacy of their immediate religious family, participants discover how to name and confront the shadow side of their religious legacies. After individual groups search the dark corners of their own traditions, they are better equipped to recognize the distinctiveness of the other's home. As one study group member noted, "I had to discover the peculiar grammar of my own faith before I realized that my neighbor was speaking a different language." During the last three years, this preparation has enabled us to explore our differences with greater sensitivity and to recognize the possibilities and limits with which each group must contend.

The preliminary task was to examine those factors that led Christians and Jews to part company in the early centuries, to trace the subsequent history, and then to unravel the contemporary theological tangles in which Christians and Jews are each caught. While the curricula were different for the Christian and Jewish groups, all participants were introduced to recent scholarship in the field of Jewish-Christian studies and encouraged to work through a similar sequence of topics and reading. To supplement these study sessions and to provide an educational forum for the larger public, the ICJS invited internationally recognized scholars to participate in workshops and to deliver lectures. While these events attracted significant crowds, our desire to engage new audiences has led to several innovative programs.

The approach is illustrated by a symposium sponsored with the Baltimore Choral Arts Society in the spring of 1991. After a year of anticipation, Tom Hall, the music director, realized an ambitious dream to perform Bach's masterpiece, *The Saint Matthew Passion.* However sublime the music, Mr. Hall recognized that a polemical edge is embedded in Matthew's Gospel which continues to pose a significant challenge for Christians and Jews. In cooperation with the Baltimore Choral Arts Society, the ICJS was awarded a grant from the Maryland Humanities Council to orchestrate a symposium designed to investigate the relationship between the arts and religious intolerance.

Dr. Jaroslav Pelikan, Sterling Professor of History at Yale University, rooted the problem of Christian anti-Judaism in a tradition of interpretation which grew out of the soil of Matthew's Gospel. As the Church struggled to establish its identity, tensions mounted and tempers flared. Negative images were deployed which later became embedded in western literature, art, and music. Dr. Robert P. Bergman, then Director of the Walters Art Gallery in Baltimore, graphically illustrated subsequent developments by reviewing the stereotypes of Judaism which have pervaded western art and were enshrined on the very portals of Christian cathedrals. As the sculptures from the Strasbourg Cathedral demonstrate, the image of the Church triumphant was juxtaposed in dramatic contrast with the blind and defeated synagogue. A chilling sequence of images was displayed to show how the fantasy of a Jewish conspiracy assumed visual expression in the fourteenth and fifteenth centuries. This portrait of the demonized Jew penetrated the western imagination and worked its dreadful magic in the Christian populace. While Dr. Eric Chafe, Associate Professor of Music at Brandeis University and a Bach scholar, noted the dangerous undercurrents of Luther's invectives, he maintained that Luther's theology of the Cross provides a critical corrective to a Church which has often projected it own failings onto the Jewish people. This piety encourages introspective confrontation and repentance and lies at the heart of Bach's creation. Dr. Eugene Fisher, Associate Director of the Secretariat for Ecumenical and Interreligious Affairs of the National Conference of Catholic Bishops, augmented these efforts in an introductory essay and an exegetical commentary on the Matthean text which placed troublesome passages in their historical context. The annotations were featured in the program notes distributed to the entire audience.

This initiative was designed to expose the subtlety of our prejudices so that we might look and listen to our artistic heritage with greater care. We are quick to notice the bigot who has little to hold onto but his hate. We readily detect the fanatic who struggles to overcome doubt by destroying its carriers. Yet we seldom recognize the extent to which we ourselves are caught in the grip of misconceptions. To identify the distortions in our own worldview, we may have to examine those sacred commitments and aesthetic affections which in large part govern the imagination. Such an enterprise raises ticklish questions and involves unsettling risks.

At one end of the spectrum, critics have argued that even the greatest artistic masterpieces must be restricted or censored if such productions disseminate misunderstandings and unwittingly sanction prejudice. In contrast, others have contended that efforts to track down and expose ideological defects engender suspicions which easily grow into hysteria. When a work of art is subjected to intensive analysis, its capacity to inspire and uplift us rarely survives. Beauty is buried in the rubble of the deconstructed artifact.

The performance of Bach's masterpiece provided our community with the opportunity to ponder serious issues from a variety of perspectives. What criteria do we invoke when we judge our most hallowed traditions, when we evaluate our most treasured creations? Can we educate ourselves so that we are immunized from infectious distortions, yet alive and responsive to the power of the work? How are we to weigh the claims of religion and art when they rest uneasily in the balance? Though the symposium neither promised nor delivered resolution to these troublesome questions, a segment of the Baltimore community which previously segregated religion and the arts began to wrestle with a conundrum that has significant ramifications.

The roots of this inquiry can be traced back to the Ninth National Workshop. The Institute's experiment in religious education has provided a forum where people struggle with their traditions, where people learn to respect one another in the midst of intense disagreement, and where the interplay of democratic and religious values is examined with rigor and passion. When we began, the ICJS board anticipated a life span of four or five years. The plan was to draw Jews and Christians out of their solitary confinement and to move the challenge of religious pluralism onto their agendas. While relationships have evolved which have proven immensely enriching, no other community organization has the resources to sustain the momentum of the ICJS. Local denominations are stretched thin by internal demands. Schools and universities are bound by academic and administrative constraints. Clergy are burdened with pastoral claims that leave little time to shoulder the additional administrative demands of an interfaith program. After surveying the landscape, the ICJS board unanimously decided that the work is vitally important not only to our own region but to other communities as well, and they have doubled their efforts to carry the initiative forward.

As Christians and Jews become better grounded in their own traditions, the ICJS will provide more opportunities for interchange. A sampling of the projects which these study groups have already developed is cited in the chart at the end of this Appendix. During the coming years, the ICJS will continue to work with both local and national leaders from the Christian and Jewish communities, coordinate programs with seminaries, and design study materials for use in schools, dialogue groups, and congregations. We will host gatherings in which Christians and Jews, clergy and laity can read and interpret texts form the Hebrew Scriptures that are read during the High Holy Days, Passover, Christmas and Easter. These study sessions will enable participants to discover the distinct ways in which we appropriate the Bible and will sensitize us to interpretations which are purchased at the other's expense. Our hope is that Christians and Jews will sit up and take note of the stories they tell, the hymns they sing, and that they will ponder how their celebrations and their laments not only give them definition but shape their perception of the other.

The ICJS holds fast to the challenge of translating the best in Jewish-Christian scholarship to the community at large. We will continue to engage clergy and lay leaders in conversations that investigate the points where religion, education and public policy converge. Though many Christians and Jews come to the table with different expectations, our hope is that each will learn how to speak across the ethnic and theological divisions. There is a growing cadre of people in this community and around the country who recognize that we cannot degrade the integrity and religious dignity of others and pretend that it does not have dangerous consequences. Unless we learn to contend with our deepest differences and build mutual trust in the midst of our disagreements, the conflicts which are polarizing our communities will escalate until they undermine the values that make a democracy possible. The conflicts that are raging around the globe provide impressive evidence to support the cynic and the tyrant. The experiment in interfaith dialogue may only offer fragile resistance. Yet a dialogue that inspires the imagination to scale the walls of hatred sustains the hope that the world is not beyond repair.

INSTITUTE FOR CHRISTIAN AND JEWISH STUDIES
A SAMPLING OF DENOMINATIONAL STUDY GROUP PROJECTS

Southern Baptist   Rev. David Yeager researched and wrote a history of Southern Baptist-Jewish relations in which he identifies issues for further study and discussion.

Roman Catholic   Dr. Rosann Catalana, theologian in residence at Mercy High School, conducted a pilot project for the Archdiocese of Baltimore. A series of seminars on Jewish-Christian studies provided the religion faculty with a new angle to assess their curriculum.

Rev. Robert Albright, Towson State chaplain, initiated a project in which he evaluates the Christian perception of Judaism reflected in hymns. He is composing liturgical alternatives which present a more positive outlook, and will hold a conference of Christian and Jewish liturgical musicians to discuss the project.

Episcopal   The group wrote and published a primer on Jewish-Christian dialogue to introduce congregations to fundamental questions and challenges confronting the church today.

Rev. William Rich, Goucher College chaplain, designed a curriculum for Jewish and Christian college students to investigate the challenge of Jewish-Christian relations and explore perceptions of one another.

Jewish   The Baltimore Board of Rabbis is engaged in a three-year study of the history of Jewish-Christian theological debate, Jewish perceptions of Christianity past and present, and Jewish misunderstandings of Christian Scripture and belief.

Lutheran   The group developed a resolution calling for study and re-evaluation of understanding of Judaism and the Jewish people by the Evangelical Lutheran Church of America.

The ICJS is planning a conference for prominent national Lutheran and Presbyterian clergy and educators to explore the history and theological impact of Jewish-Christian relations on the contemporary Church. Participants will learn how to use teaching materials prepared by the ICJS for Congregational Adult Education.

Methodist   Rev. Roberta Scoville wrote a guide for Christian Bible Study based on the dialogical model of the Rabbinic *Beit Midrash*.

Presbyterian   Members of this group conducted seminars around the Baltimore Presbytery to engage clergy and leaders in the contemporary issues of Jewish-Christian relations.

Rev. Jack Sharp edited commentaries by seventeen renowned scholars on the pitfalls of anti-Judaic interpretations which arise in the lectionary cycle from Palm Sunday to Easter. These notes were broadcast on the Ecunet computer service to the U.S. and Canada for use by clergy in sermon preparation and to encourage a more sensitive understanding of the problematic scriptural texts.

A General Bibliography on Jewish-Christian Relations

Eugene J. Fisher

GENERAL RESOURCES

Lawrence Boadt, Helga Croner, Leon Klenicki, eds., **Biblical Studies: Meeting Ground of Jews and Christians** (Paulist/Stimulus, 1980).
Trends in biblical interpretation and clarification of misinterpretation.

James H. Charlesworth, editor. **Jews and Christians Exploring the Past, Present and Future** (Crossroad, 1990); **Jesus' Jewishness: Exploring the Place of Jesus within Early Judaism** (Crossroad, 1991); **Overcoming Fear between Jews and Christians** (Crossroad, 1993).
Jewish and Christian scholars probe the causes of mistrust from biblical times to the present and suggest means of developing mutual esteem.

Helga Croner, editor. **Stepping Stones to Further Jewish-Christian Relations** (Paulist/Stimulus, 1977); **More Stepping Stones** (Paulist/Stimulus 1985).
These two volumes contain the statements of Protestant and Catholic Church bodies on Christian-Jewish relations.

Eugene J. Fisher. **Faith Without Prejudice: Rebuilding Christian Attitudes toward Jews and Judaism** (Crossroad, 1993); **Seminary Education and Christian-Jewish Relations** (National Catholic Educational Association, 1988); **Interwoven Destinies: Jews and Christians Through the Ages** (Paulist/Stimulus, 1993); with Leon Klenicki, **John Paul II on Jews and Judaism 1979-1986** (U.S. Catholic Conference, 1987).

Edward J. Flannery. **The Anguish of the Jews: Twenty-Three Centuries of Antisemitism** (Paulist, 1985).
An historical survey of Christian antisemitism by a Catholic author.

John Rousmaniere. **A Bridge to Dialogue: The Story of Jewish-Christian Relations** (Paulist/Stimulus, 1991).
Popular historical and contemporary overview of the relationship.

M. Shermis and A. Zannoni, eds. **Introduction to Jewish-Christian Relations** (Paulist, 1991).
Basic essays on scripture, the Holocaust, Israel, antisemitism, Jesus and the Pharisees, intermarriage, feminism and religious pluralism.

J. Spiro and H. Hirsch, eds. **Persistent Prejudice** (George Mason Univ. Press, 1988).
Essays on the history of antisemitism.

Clark M. Williamson. **When Jews and Christians Meet: A Guide for Christian Preaching and Teaching** (CBP Press, 1989).
A Protestant perspective for preachers and teachers.

_____ ed. **A Mutual Witness: Toward Critical Solidarity between Jews and Christians** (Chalice Press, 1992).

BEGINNINGS: ROOTS AND BRANCHES

Roger Brooks and John Collins, eds. **Hebrew Bible or Old Testament? Studying the Bible in Judaism and Christianity** (Univ. of Notre Dame Press, 1990).
How Jews and Christians read the same texts differently.

Philip Cunningham. **Jewish Apostle to The Gentiles: Paul as He Saw Himself** (Twenty-Third Publications, 1986).
Excellent summary on a popular level of the results of recent Pauline studies.

Alan T. Davies, ed. **Anti-Semitism and the Foundations of Christianity** (Paulist, 1979).
Twelve top scholars survey recent studies.

David Efroymson, E. Fisher, L. Klenicki, eds. **Within Context: Essays On Jews and Judaism in the New Testament** (Liturgical Press, 1993).
Aids for teachers, preachers and adult Christians in reading the New Testament free of prejudice toward Jews and Judaism.

Eugene J. Fisher, ed. **The Jewish Roots of Christian Liturgy** (Paulist, 1990).

_____ and Leon Klenicki. **Root and Branches: Biblical Judaism, Rabbinic Judaism and Early Christianity** (St. Mary's Press, 1987).

Lloyd Gaston. **Paul and the Torah** (Univ. of British Columbia Press, 1987). An innovative scholarly approach to the Pauline texts.

Daniel J. Harrington. **God's People in Christ** (Fortress, 1980). Essays on the New Testament.

_____. **Paul on the mystery of Israel** (Liturgical Press/Michael Glazier, 1992). A popular guide to the Pauline texts relevant to Christian understanding of Judaism, and to the major scholarly debates surrounding them.

Michael Hilton and Gordian Marshall, O.P. **The Gospels and Rabbinic Judaism: A Study Guide** (KTAV/ADL, 1988). Takes the reader through parallel texts from the New Testament and the Talmud.

Jon D. Levenson. **The Hebrew Bible, the Old Testament, and Historical Criticism** (Westminster/John Knox Press, 1993). The use and abuse of historical critical methodology in biblical studies.

Norbert Lohfink. **The Covenant Never Revoked: Biblical Reflections on Christian-Jewish Dialogue** (Paulist, 1991). Twelve provocative theses providing new approaches to the New Testament texts on Jews and Judaism.

Hayim Goren Perelmuter. **Siblings: Rabbinic Judaism and Early Christianity at Their Beginnings** (Paulist, 1989). Presents a theory of the relationship in its origins; presents and examines numerous rabbinic texts.

E.P. Sanders. **Jesus and Judaism** (Fortress, 1985); and **Jewish Law from Jesus to the Mishnah** (SCM/Trinity, 1990). Scholarly and well worth the effort.

George M. Smiga. **Pain and Polemic: Anti-Judaism in the Gospels** (Paulist/Stimulus, 1992).

Tight, very helpful analysis of the polemical passages of the New Testament by a Catholic scholar.

Geza Vermes. **The Religion of Jesus the Jew** (Fortress, 1993).
A leading Jewish scholar sketches Jesus' teaching, preaching and practice of the law, healing and prayer.

Clark M. Williamson and Ronald J. Allen. **Interpreting Difficult Texts: Anti-Judaism and Christian Preaching** (SCM/Trinity, 1989)
Protestant parallel to the Smiga volume.

THE PARTING OF THE WAYS

Paul F. Bradshaw and Lawrence A. Hoffman, eds. **The Making of Jewish and Christian Worship** (Univ. of Notre Dame Press, 1991).
Scholars explore the origin and growth of Christian and Jewish liturgies from the first century when both rabbinic Judaism and Christianity were defining themselves separately and in relationship to each other.

John G. Gager. **The Origins of Anti-Semitism** (Oxford Univ. Press, 1983).
Study of Patristic literature.

Val A. McInnes, O.P., ed. **New Visions: Historical and Theological Perspectives on the Jewish-Christian Dialogue** (Crossroad, 1993).
Essays on the early centuries of Jewish-Christian relations by Sean Freyne, Robert Wilken and Jakob Petuchowski (on the Our Father) and on contemporary re-evaluations by Jurgen Moltmann, Lawrence Frizzel, John Macquarrie, and David Jenkins.

Leon Poliakov. **The History of Anti-Semitism** (Vanguard, 1976).
Four volumes. Classic text offering a chronological approach through the ages.

Marc Saperstein. **Moments of Crisis in Jewish-Christian Relations** (SCM/Trinity, 1990).
Short, probing essays on the periods of Antiquity, the Middle Ages, the Reformation, and the present from a Jewish point of view.

Robert L. Wilken. **Judaism and the Early Christian Mind** (Yale Univ. Press, 1971).

_____. **John Crysostom and the Jews: Rhetoric and Reality in the Late Fourth Century** (Berkeley, 1983).

_____. with Wayne Meeks. **Jews, Christians in Antioch in the First Four Centuries of the Common Era** (Scholars Press, 1978).

_____. **The Land Called Holy: Palestine in Christian History and Thought** (Yale Univ. Press, 1993).
Evokes the Christian conception of a "Holy Land" as first a place of pilgrimage and then a place to live, and Jewish responses to Christians living in the land up to the Muslim conquest of Jerusalem in the seventh century.

THE MEDIEVAL PERIOD

Jeremy Cohen. **The Friars and the Jews: The Evolution of Medieval Anti-Judaism** (Cornell Univ. Press, 1982).
Though somewhat controversial, illustrates the qualitatively different and much less tolerant atmosphere that developed in medieval Christendom and after the First Crusade in 1096 saw the first great massacres of Jews by Christians.

F.E. Peters. **Children of Abraham: Judaism, Christianity, Islam** (Princeton Univ. Press, 1982); and **Judaism, Christianity and Islam: The Classical Texts and Their Interpretation,** three volumes (Princeton Univ. Press, 1990).
Together, these volumes form perhaps the best and most insightful comparative study of the origins, interconnections, parallels and differences between the three "Abrahamic" traditions in their origins and early interaction.

Kenneth R. Stow. **Catholic Thought and Papal Jewish Policy** (Jewish Theological Seminary, 1977).
Again, reveals the surprising complexity and protectiveness of papal policy.

Edward A. Synan. **The Popes and the Jews in the Middle Ages** (Macmillan, 1965).
Letting the chips fall where they may, Synan presents relevant Church texts and their historical contexts.

F.E. Talmage. **Disputation and Dialogue** (ADL/KTAV, 1975).
Texts and commentary from over the ages. Remains a basic reader.

Joshua Trachtenberg. **The Devil and the Jews: The Medieval Conception of the Jew** (ADL/Jewish Publication Society, 1983).
Marc Saperstein's Introduction for this edition points out that Trachtenberg presents a true but incomplete picture of the period. The tolerant and even positive policies displayed toward the Jews by the Church in the Middle Ages need also to be told.

Y.H. Yerushalmi, et. al. **Bibliographical Essays in Medieval Jewish Studies** (ADL/KTAV, 1976).
Contains an excellent essay on "The Church and the Jews" by Kenneth R. Stow. ADL's earlier volume in the series (1972) has an insightful essay by Frank Talmage on "Judaism on Christianity: Christianity on Judaism."

REFORMATION AND ENLIGHTMENT

John Edwards. **The Jews in Christian Europe, 1400-1700** (Routledge, 1988).
Excellent survey of the history of the transition from the medieval world to the eve of the Enlightment.

Arthur Hertzberg. **The French Enlightenment and the Jews** (Columbia Univ. Press, 1985).
New classic text revealing that in some ways the "enlightened" thinkers held darker and more racist views of Jews and Judaism than their medieval or Reformation predecessors.

Heiko Oberman. **The Roots of Anti-Semitism in the Ages of Renaissance and Reformation** (Fortress, 1984).
Erasmus, Reuchlin, Pfefferkorn, Calvin, Luther and others.

THE CONTEMPORARY DIALOGUE

Paul F. Bradshaw and Lawrence A. Hoffman, eds. **The Changing Face of Jewish and Christian Worship in North America** (Univ. of Notre Dame Press, 1991).
Contains essays delineating major contemporary liturgical changes, including the images of the other projected in Jewish and Christian liturgy.

David Burrell and Yehezkel Landau, eds. **Voices from Jerusalem** (Paulist/Stimulus, 1992).
Jews and Christians who live there reflect on the Holy Land.

Martin A. Cohen and Helga Croner. **Christian Mission/Jewish Mission** (Paulist/Stimulus, 1982).
Historical and contemporary theological reflections.

Alice and Roy Eckardt. **Long Night's Journey into Day: Life and Faith After the Holocaust** (Wayne State Univ. Press, 1982).

_____. **Jews and Christians: The Contemporary Meeting** (Wayne State Univ. Press, 1986).

Eugene J. Fisher and James Rudin, eds. **Twenty Years of Jewish-Catholic Relations** (Paulist, 1986).
Essays by leading figures in the American dialogue since Vatican II on the Council, liturgy, Israel, education and the Shoah.

_____ and Leon Klenicki. **In Our Time: The Flowering of Jewish-Catholic Dialogue** (Paulist/Stimulus, 1990).
Key documents and commentary of the dialogue. Fifty-page annotated bibliography-essay on the literature in the field.

_____ and Daniel Polish, eds. **Social Policy in the Catholic and Jewish Traditions:** Vol. 1: *Formation*; Vol. 2. *Liturgical Foundations* (Univ. of Notre Dame Press, 1980, 1981).
Papers from consultations between the Synagogue Council of America and the National Conference of Catholic Bishops.

International Catholic-Jewish Liaison Committee. **Fifteen years of Catholic-Jewish Dialogue, 1970-1985.** (Libreria Editrice Lateranense and Libreria Editrice Vaticana, 1988).

Steven J. Jacobs, ed. **Contemporary Jewish and Christian Responses to the Shoah** (Univ. Press of America, 1993).
Two volumes (one "Jewish," one "Christian") carefully selected to be representative and provocative.

Anthony Kenny. **Catholics, Jews and the Land of Israel** (Paulist/Stimulus, 1993).
The best statement to date of contemporary theological and official Catholic attitudes toward the rebirth of a Jewish State in Eretz Israel.

Leon Klenicki, ed. **Toward A Theological Encounter: Jewish Understandings of Christianity** (Paulist/Stimulus, 1991).
Eight major Jewish scholars involved in the dialogue reflect on how Jewish thought might take results of the dialogue into account.

Franklin H. Littell. **The Crucifixion of the Jews** (Harper and Row, 1975).
Reflections of one of the pioneers of Holocaust studies.

David Novak. **Jewish-Christian Dialogue: A Jewish Justification** (Oxford Univ. Press, 1989).
Philosophical approaches to dialogue.

John Pawlikowski. **Jesus and the Theology of Israel** (Michael Glazier, 1989).
Excellent survey of the scholarly discussion to date.

A. James Rudin. **Israel for Christians** (Fortress, 1982).
Excellent popular introduction to Zionism and what the State of Israel means to the Jewish people religiously and sociologically.

_____ and Marvin Wilson. **A Time to Speak: The Evangelical-Jewish Encounter** (Eerdmans, 1987).

The Theology of the Churches and the Jewish People: Statements of the World Council of Churches and Its Member Churches (WCC Publications, 1988), with commentaries by Alan Brockway, Paul van Buren, Rolf Rentdorff, and Simon Schoon.

Clems Thoma and Michael Wyschogrod, eds. **Understanding Scripture** and **Parable and Story in Judaism and Christianity** (Paulist/Stimulus, 1987) and 1989).
Explorations of Rabbinic and Christian traditions of biblical interpretation and narrative.

Paul van Buren. **A Theology of the Jewish-Christian Reality.** Four volumes: Vols. 1-3 (Seabury, 1976, 1980, 1983); Vol. 4 (Harper and Row, 1988).
Major attempt to rethink Christian systematic theology in the light of the Church's dialogue with the Jewish people.

Johannes Cardinal Willebrands. **Church and Jewish People: New Considerations** (Paulist, 1992).
Major addresses and essays by one of the architects of the Second Vatican

Council's Declaration on the Jews, *Nostra Aetate, No. 4,* and the president of the Pontifical Council for Religious Relations with the Jews from 1969 to 1989.

Clark M. Williamson. **A Guest In the House of Israel: Post-Holocaust Church Theology** (Westminster/John Knox, 1993).
A provocative attempt to reconstruct Christian theology from a Protestant perspective in the light of the searching critique to which examination of its anti-Jewish past subjects it.

Alfred Wolf and Royale Vadakin, eds. **A Journey of Discovery: A Resource Manual for Jewish-Catholic Dialogue** (Tabor, 1989).
Handy, loose-leaf format includes joint statements and resources developed by the Los Angeles Respect Life, Priest-Rabbi, and Women's Dialogue groups over the course of two decades. A valuable resource.

JOURNALS

Explorations: Rethinking Relationships Among Jews and Christians. Published occasionally and gratis by the American Interfaith Institute (401 North Broad St., Philadelphia, PA 19108). Popular-level updates mainly on biblical issues.

Focus on Interfaith. Published twice yearly by the Intergroup Relations Division of the Anti-Defamation League of B'nai B'rith (823 United Nations Plaza, New York, NY 10017–3560).

Journal of Ecumenical Studies (Philadelphia: Temple University).
In addition to in-depth articles, JES regularly abstracts from journals and reports events from around the world.

National Dialogue Newsletter. Published quarterly for local dialogue groups (301 Godfrey Road, Fairfield, CT 06430).

The SIDIC Review. Published in Rome by the Sisters of Sion, is devoted exclusively to matters related to the Jewish-Christian dialogue. Its topical issues make is especially useful for teachers, as well as those wishing to keep current with regard to events, documents, etc. Contact the Secretariat for Ecumenical and Interreligious Affairs of the National Conference of Catholic Bishops (3211 Fourth Street, N.E., Washington, D.C. 20017-1194) for information on subscriptions.

Notes on the Contributors

DR. EUGENE FISHER is the Director of Catholic-Jewish Relations for the National conference of Catholic Bishops. A leading international advocate of dialogue, his efforts have implemented far-reaching changes in the life of the Church, its teaching and practice. He is author or editor of numerous volumes, including *Faith Without Prejudice* (1992); *Twenty Years of Jewish-Catholic Relations* (1986); and *Jewish Roots of Christian Liturgy* (1990). He is a Consultor to the Holy See's Commission for Religious Relations with the Jewish People and a member of the International Catholic-Jewish Liaison Committee.

RABBI IRVING GREENBERG is the President and co-founder of CLAL: The National Jewish Center for Learning and Leadership. He is active in interfaith dialogue and the leading figure in intra-Jewish dialogue. He has also been a seminal thinker in confronting the Holocaust and in viewing Israel as the Jewish assumption of power and the beginning of the third era in Jewish history. Rabbi Greenberg is the author of *The Jewish Way: Living the Holidays* (1988).

RABBI DAVID HARTMAN, Ph.D., Founder and Director of the Shalom Hartman Institute of Jerusalem, is widely hailed as one of the most profound Jewish philosophers of contemporary times. A two-time winner of the prestigious National Jewish book Award for *Maimonides* in 1976 and *A Living Covenant* in 1986, Dr. Hartman has dedicated his actions and scholarship to the promotion of traditional Judaism as a viable spiritual option for our modern world.

FATHER JOHN T. PAWLIKOWSKI, O.S.M. is Professor of Social Ethics at The Catholic Theological Union of Chicago. His books include *Christ in the Light of the Christian-Jewish Dialogue* (1982) and *Jesus and the Theology of Israel* (1989). He is a member of the Advisory Committee for Catholic-Jewish Relations of the National Conference of Catholic Bishops and the U.S. Holocaust Memorial Council.

REV. DR. PAUL M. VAN BUREN is Professor Emeritus at Temple University and has written numerous articles and seven books, including *Discerning the Way* (1980) and *A Christian Theology of the People Israel* (3 vols., 1983-1988). He has served since 1980 on the World Council of Churches' Consultation on the Church and the Jewish People.

Index

Clemens Thoma and Michael Wyschogrod, editors, *Parable and Story in Judaism and Christianity* (A Stimulus Book, 1989).

Eugene J. Fisher and Leon Klenicki, editors, *In Our Time: The Flowering of Jewish-Catholic Dialogue* (A Stimulus Book, 1990).

Leon Klenicki, editor, *Toward A Theological Encounter* (A Stimulus Book, 1991).

David Burrell and Yehezkel Landau, editors, *Voices from Jerusalem* (A Stimulus Book, 1991).

John Rousmaniere, *A Bridge to Dialogue: The Story of Jewish-Christian Relations;* edited by James A. Carpenter and Leon Klenicki (A Stimulus Book, 1991).

Michael E. Lodahl, *Shekhinah/Spirit* (A Stimulus Book, 1992)

George M. Smiga, *Pain and Polemic: Anti-Judaism in the Gospels* (A Stimulus Book, 1992).

Eugene J. Fisher, editor, *Interwoven Destinies: Jews and Christians Through the Ages* (A Stimulus Book, 1993).

Anthony Kenny, *Catholics, Jews and the State of Israel* (A Stimulus Book, 1993).

STIMULUS BOOKS are developed by Stimulus Foundation, a not-for-profit organization, and are published by Paulist Press. The Foundation wishes to further the publication of scholarly books on Jewish and Christian topics that are of importance to Judaism and Christianity.

Stimulus Foundation was established by an erstwhile refugee from Nazi Germany who intends to contribute with these publications to the improvement of communication between Jews and Christians.

Books for publication in this Series will be selected by a committee of the Foundation, and offers of manuscripts and works in progress should be addressed to:

Stimulus Foundation
c/o Paulist Press
997 Macarthur Boulevard
Mahwah, N.J. 07430